GILBERT KEITH CHESTERTON was born at Campden Hill, London on 29th May 1874. He was educated at St Paul's School (where he started a magazine, *The Debater*) and the Slade School of Art. He married in 1901 and produced two volumes of verse. In 1904 he wrote *The Napoleon of Notting Hill* and followed this with studies of *Dickens* (1906) and *Robert Browning* (1909). He then wrote two works reflecting his religious and social beliefs and in 1911 the first in a series of detective stories, *The Innocence of Father Brown*, was published. In 1916 he took over the editorship of the *New Witness* from his brother and in 1922 was received into the Roman Catholic Church by his friend Father O'Connor, the original of 'Father Brown'. In the course of a busy life as journalist, author and lecturer, he produced over 100 volumes, including various religious writings, poetry and essays as well as illustrating the novels of his friend, Hilaire Belloc. He died in 1936.

MICHAEL SLATER is Professor of Victorian Literature at Birkbeck College in the University of London, a former editor of *The Dickensian* and a past President of the Dickens Fellowship. He is the author of several books and articles on Dickens, including *Dickens and Women* (1983).

G. K. CHESTERTON

Criticisms & Appreciations of the Works of Charles Dickens

Introduction by Michael Slater
*Professor of Victorian Literature
at Birkbeck College in the University of London*

J. M. Dent & Sons Ltd:
London
Charles E. Tuttle Co., Inc.
Rutland, Vermont
EVERYMAN'S LIBRARY

Introduction © J. M. Dent & Co. 1992

*Appreciations and Criticisms of the Works of
Charles Dickens* by G. K. Chesterton first
published in Everyman's Library in 1911,
reprinted 1933.

All rights reserved.

Printed in Great Britain by
The Guernsey Press Co. Ltd, Guernsey, C.I.
for
J. M. Dent & Sons Ltd
91 Clapham High St
London SW4 7TA
and
Charles E. Tuttle Co., Inc.
28 South Main Street
Rutland, Vermont 05701
USA

British Library Cataloguing in Publication Data
is available upon request

ISBN 0 460 87084 X

Everyman's Library
Reg. U.S. Patent Office

CONTENTS

vi   Contents

INTRODUCTION

Chesterton's figure bulks large (very much the *cliché juste* in this case) not only in the crowded history but also in the teeming present of Dickens criticism. T.S.Eliot wrote in 1932, 'there is no better critic of Dickens living than Mr Chesterton', and Peter Ackroyd has observed in his recent, masterly, Dickens biography, that Chesterton is 'perhaps Dickens's best critic', an observation to which proper weight can be given only when it is realised that Mr Ackroyd has evidently read virtually everything ever written about Dickens. He has certainly read everything Chesterton ever wrote about Dickens. Most readers, however, will know only Chesterton's *Charles Dickens,* seldom out of print for long since its first publication in 1906, and maybe also his comments on Dickens in *The Victorian Age in Literature* (1913) where the rise of Dickens is likened to 'the rising of a vast mob' and his art is memorably defined as by Chesterton as 'that most exquisite of arts . . . the art of enjoying everybody'. The series of introductions to individual Dickens titles that Chesterton wrote for Everyman's Library in 1907 and 1909 remain comparatively unknown even though, as we might expect, they contain far more in the way of detailed commentary on particular books than can be found in the 1906 volume.

Chesterton's passionate public engagement with Dickens
dates, in fact, from the first year of this century when, in a
Bookman article, he contrasted two paintings of Dickens in
the National Portrait Gallery and in so doing made quite
clear just what it was in Dickens's work that he deplored
and what, on a much larger scale, he gloried in. The 1839
Maclise portrait of a 'languid, fashionable and rather under-
bred young man, with repulsively long hair' shows, he
declared, the 'refuse of the soul of Dickens': it shows us
'the man who wrote the repentance of Dombey and the
death of Little Nell, not the man who wrote of Todgers's
boarding-house and Bob Sawyer's party'. The later portrait
by Ary Scheffer, on the other hand, shows us 'what Dickens
really was': 'a brisk vivid-looking man . . . with the open
and almost hungry eyes of the natural humorist, and the
firm-set, almost insolent mouth and chin which mark the
self-made man who is something better than a gentleman'.
For Chesterton the essential greatness of Dickens as man
and as artist was always to be found in his laughter, the
great comic scenes and characters that abound most richly
in his earlier novels. Dickens's weakness lay in the kind of
'vulgar' sentimentality that brings the reader tidings of
comfort rather than joy, cosy 'happy endings' or the soothing
apotheosis of Little Nell, rather than the hilarious triumphs
of the human spirit exemplified by such 'inexhaustible'
characters as Sam Weller, Mrs Nickleby, Dick Swiveller,
Mr Toots or Mr Micawber.

Born in Kensington in 1874, almost exactly four years
after Dickens's death, the young Chesterton seems to have
felt himself as living in the immediate afterglow of a high
Victorian noonday, and as having a special connection to
Dickens in that a recent forebear of his father's, the re-

forming prison governor, Captain George Laval Chesterton, had been a friend of Dickens's and, says Chesterton in his *Autobiography*, 'I suspect, himself something of a Dickens character'. He goes on to say that his earliest memories and the stories he heard from his father suggested to him 'that there were a good many characters in the days of Dickens', all part of what he called the 'Great Gusto' that 'breathed out of that epoch; something now only remembered in the rich and rollicking quotations of Swiveller and Micawber'. When, after a conventional middle-class education at St Paul's School, and a period at University College London, which he left without taking a degree, Chesterton gravitated towards the literary world in the mid 1890's, he reacted strongly against the prevalent atmosphere he found there: 'My first impulse to write', he later declared, . . . was a revolt of disgust with the Decadents and the aesthetic pessimism of the 'nineties'. Nor did he find the prevailing political fashions any more acceptable than the artistic ones. Brought up in a family he characterised as 'the best sort of middle-Victorian Liberals', Chesterton found the Socialism of the Webbs and the Imperialism of Kipling equally objectionable. By the time he was beginning to make his way on the newspaper first edited by Dickens himself, *The Daily News*, he had become notorious as a vociferous opponent of the Boer War. He soon had his regular weekly column on the *News* and was a frequent reviewer for and contributor to *The Bookman*. Here in 1903 he published his first substantial appreciation of Dickens, celebrating above all his subject's zestful, superabundant creativity and his tonic optimism.

In the same year Chesterton was invited to contribute a volume on Browning, another great Victorian master of the literary grotesque, to Macmillan's 'English Men of Letters' series. The book 'created a sensation', wrote Chesterton's first biographer, Maisie Ward. He triumphantly exposed the fatuity of criticising Browning's poetry for not being like Tennyson's and, as Ward puts it, 'claimed Browning as a poet not for experts but for every man'. He set himself to de-mystify the poetry and reveal its special glories for all to enjoy. As with his Dickens criticism, though, there is no question of undiscriminating panegyric: he clearly perceives the faults that can result from Browning's fondness for ellipsis, for example, his 'kind of insane swiftness'. And he notes that Browning, like almost all original stylists, is 'subject to one most disastrous habit – the habit of writing imitations of [himself]'. This last criticism is one very often levelled at Chesterton himself, of course, – for example by W.H.Auden, in his admiring Introduction to his 1970 selection from Chesterton's non-fictional prose, where he blames it on the pressures of that journalism to which Chesterton was addicted:

> When he is really enthralled by a subject he is brilliant, without any doubt one of the finest aphorists in English literature, but, when his imagination is not fully held he can write an exasperating parody of himself, and this is most likely to happen when he has a dead-line to meet.

Chesterton's imagination was certainly very fully held by Browning and, still more, by Dickens. By the time he came to write his book-length study *Charles Dickens* in 1906 he had himself published his first novel, *The Napoleon of Notting Hill,* a fantasy of the future with a strong dash of Chesterton's beloved medievalism. It enabled him to dramatise many of his deepest beliefs and most cherished hatreds (Notting Hill becomes an imperial power, attempting to lord it over other London boroughs) and further consolidated his position as one of the most popular writers of the day.

Before the publication of Chesterton's *Dickens* the most substantial and influential study to have appeared was George Gissing's *Charles Dickens* (1898) and Chesterton's book is, among other things, a riposte to Gissing who laid too much emphasis, Chesterton thought, upon the sadder and harsher elements to be found in Dickens's work. It has been said that Gissing gives us 'the thin man's Dickens and Chesterton the fat man's Dickens' and there is indeed a certain broad truth in this, though Gissing shows plenty of keen appreciation of Dickens's supreme comic gifts and Chesterton, more especially perhaps in the Everyman Introductions reprinted here, shows plenty of awareness of, and responsiveness to, the darker side of Dickens's genius, what he calls on p.40 his 'other kind of energy, horrible, uncanny, barbaric'.

Chesterton's *Dickens* is cast in a quasi-biographical mould, with chapters on his boyhood, youth, the writing of *Pickwick*, his 1842 visit to America and so on but nothing could be further from the kind of biography that Auden characterised as 'the shilling life [which] will give you all the facts'. Chesterton was concerned only with those details of Dickens's life that seemed to him to point to some fundamental quality in the man. 'Some of the earliest glimpses we have of Charles Dickens,' he notes, 'show him to us perched on some chair or table singing comic songs in an atmosphere of perpetual applause' and as a result 'there did mingle with his merits all his life this theatrical quality, this atmosphere of being shown off – a sort of hilarious self-consciousness'. An observation like this is worth whole volumes of scrupulously piled-up scholarly facts in helping us to get some insight into the phenomenon that was Dickens, just as his perception that 'it is characteristic of Dickens that his atmospheres are more important than his stories' directs us to something that lies at the very heart of Dickens's art, a quality that Chesterton suggests is essentially visionary in nature.

In his book Chesterton made some very questionable statements about Dickens's life (for example, that he had 'got hold of the wrong sister' when he married Catherine Hogarth, a remark that drew a protest from Dickens's surviving daughter to whom Chesterton made a contrite visit) and some astonishing assertions about his work (for example: 'Dickens's work is to be reckoned always by characters, sometimes by groups, oftener by episodes, but never by novels'). But, more than any other commentator on Dickens before or since, he rises triumphantly to the highth of his great argument and makes us feel upon our pulses (to borrow a Keatsian phrase) the unique greatness of Dickens's art. He does this not so much by critical analysis or even by quotation and comment as by mere assertion but assertion couched in vivid language and surprising imagery that is in itself a not unworthy tribute to Dickens's own super-vivid language and utterly astonishing imagery. Here he is, for example, on Dickens's fecundity:

> One of the godlike things about Dickens is his quantity, his quantity as such, the enormous output, the incredible fecundity of his invention. I have said . . . that not one of us could have invented Mr Guppy [a comparatively minor character in *Bleak House*]. But even if we could have stolen Mr Guppy from Dickens we have still ᴜ confront the fact that Dickens would have been able to invent another quite inconceivable character to take his place. Perhaps we could have created Mr Guppy; but the effort would certainly have exhausted us; we should be ever afterwards wheeled about in a bath-chair at Bournemouth.

It is surely the absurd comic hyperbole at the end of this passage that clinches our conviction of the supreme comic quality of Mr Guppy.

After the success of Chesterton's *Charles Dickens,* it is not surprising that J.M.Dent should have approached him to write introductions to all Dickens' works for the Everyman's Library series of cheap reprints of classics of world literature. The first fifty Everymans were published in 1906 and included two Dickens titles, *Barnaby Rudge* and *A Tale of Two Cities,* with introductions by Walter Jerrold, a seemingly indefatigable late Victorian/Edwardian man of letters, but Dent, or his Everyman general editor, Ernest Rhys, must have decided to proceed towards a complete Dickens in the series and enlisted Chesterton's aid. Most of Chesterton's prefaces are dated 1907, a few 1909, and some not dated at all. All were written by 1911 when Dent's published them collected in one volume with the title *Appreciations and Criticisms of the Works of Charles Dickens* (reprinted, with the first two nouns of the title reversed, in 1933). For this volume Chesterton made a number of revisions to the original texts, mainly tightening up the style and excising passages that tended towards repetitiveness. Some further comments on *The Chimes* and also remarks on *The Cricket on the Hearth* were cut from the end of the *Christmas Books* introduction and some (happily not all) of the robust sallies against contemporary social or intellectual fashions are cut, e.g., 'One half of our upper classes is distributing cocoa for the people's good; the other half is distributing gin for its own good' (introduction to *Reprinted Pieces*). There was also more belabouring of Gissing in the *Little Dorrit* introduction than survives into the 1911 volume. Gissing's book on Dickens is called 'a really able study' but his hailing *Little Dorrit* as Dickens's greatest work is just because 'Mr Gissing is Mr Gissing. His school maintains that a man writes better if he is slightly ill.'

In 1911 Chesterton also wrote an introduction for the collected volume on to the end of which was joined his preface to *The Uncommercial Traveller* – presumably because this title had not yet appeared as a separate volume in Everyman. Like everything he ever wrote, this general introduction has many felicities, as when he says of his prefaces:

> they were harmless, being diluted by, or rather drowned in Dickens. My scrap of theory was a mere dry biscuit to be taken with the grand tawny port of great English comedy; and by most people it was not taken at all – like the biscuit.

It is not reprinted here, however, since it was mainly concerned to place Dickens in relation to such social and political concerns of 1911 as the growth of Socialism, the appearance of South African millionaires, and so on. Chesterton praises Dickens for his awareness of the fluctuating nature of the process of social change, contrasting him with Thackeray, 'that good Victorian radical' who had no idea that 'progress could ever change its direction', and then lurches into one of those passages that lay him open to the charge of anti-Semitism and that are an undeniable blemish on his reputation (however much we may blame them on the influence of Hilaire Belloc). His introduction eventually tails off into a few topical after-thoughts about some of the books, a partial restoration of his remarks about Gissing and *Dorrit,* and culminates in his fine essay on *The Uncommercial Traveller* which has been reprinted here, immediately following this Introduction.

The Prefaces themselves continue Chesterton's celebration of Dickens as joyous creator, social prophet and
glorifier of the common man. They necessarily pay more
attention to the distinctive qualities of individual works than
his book on Dickens does but, as Peter Hunt remarks in
his excellent detailed study of Chesterton's Dickens criticism
(Ph.D. thesis, Dalhousie University, 1980), Chesterton was
concerned in the prefaces:

> to say something about each novel that seemed to him most signifi-
> cant, and not to attempt a fully-rounded view of the novel or its
> plots, themes and characters.

He focuses on 'the purely romantic method' of *Nicholas
Nickleby* or on the way in which Dickens so powerfully
demonstrates in *Hard Times* that 'England had rubbed out
two words of the revolutionary motto, had left only Liberty
and destroyed Equality and Fraternity'. Sometimes his own
personal prejudices tend to distort his commentary, most
notably in the case of the essay on *David Copperfield*
where his 'Little Englanderism' is disturbed by what he
calls the 'colonial optimism' of its ending and it is unfortunate,
amusing though his discussion is, that the *Edwin Drood*
essay should centre quite so much on the obsessive
'Droodians' and their everlasting attempts to solve the
unfinished mystery. 'There seems to be no end to this
insane process', Chesterton remarks, words he may have
recalled in January 1914 when he found himself presiding as
judge over a public trial of John Jasper for the murder of
Drood. (This bizarre event was staged by the Dickens
Fellowship with the injudicious choice of Bernard Shaw for
foreman of the jury – as might have been anticipated, he
found an impish way to subvert the whole proceedings,

which had been organised with the utmost seriousness, not
to say solemnity.) Yet, even in these pieces Chesterton
still has many illuminating points to make and, as usual,
they are made all the more effectively by wit and humour.
For example, when he writes, 'I have a horrible feeling
that David Copperfield will send even his aunt to Australia
if she worries him too much about donkeys', he is, in an
unforgettable way, highlighting a certain quality in the novel
that stamps it as, in a limiting sense, 'Victorian'.

One of the great pleasures of these prefaces is
Chesterton's ability not only to find a phrase really worthy
of Dickens's major comic characters, as when he writes of
Mrs Gamp's 'unctuous and sumptuous conversation', but
also to focus on some comparatively minor character in a
brilliantly illuminating way. He will make us suddenly perceive not simply how entertaining that character is and how
skilfully presented, but also what, in the wider sense, he
or she *means*. The discussions of Mr Toots in *Dombey and
Son,* Caddy Jellyby in *Bleak House* or Trabb's boy in *Great
Expectations* are all cases in point. (The last three sentences
about Toots and how he might have been presented in a
modern 'psychological novel' on p.128 were added for the
1911 volume, incidentally. The original text was less com-
bative: 'Toots is perhaps the only man, except Dickens,
who enjoys everything that happens in the story of *Dombey
and Son.*') Only once does Chesterton seem to get such a
minor character preposterously wrong and that is when his
intense democratic sympathies cause him to see the odious
Sim Tappertit in *Barnaby Rudge* as 'a perfectly honourable
fool' a sort of Liberal revolutionary (all the discussion of
the novel's essentially 'picturesque' quality is, on the other
hand, both excellent and enlightening).

Another of the pleasures of these prefaces, and one greatly enhanced by reading them as a collection, is Chesterton's constant cross-referencing from the book under discussion to other Dickens novels, something he is able to do with special ease and authority because his knowledge of Dickens's work is like Sam Weller's of London, 'extensive and peculiar'. Not only does this help us to 'place' any particular book in Dickens's work as a whole but it also helps us to distinguish just what is unique about it. Perhaps the best example of this comes in his discussion of *Dombey and Son* as a transitional novel but the surprising comparison of the 'sad' *Little Dorrit* to the earlier picaresque novels (pp. 178-79, below) should also be particularly noted as making us suddenly register a quality in the novel that tends to be overlooked now despite all the blaze of critical attention that the book enjoys. The comparisons with Thackeray that form a sort of leitmotif throughout these prefaces are also very valuable, helping to sharpen our sense of the uniqueness of each of the two Titans of the Victorian novel. In the case of *Great Expectations* particularly the invocation of Thackeray throws light on the nature of the book itself and what Chesterton terms its 'quality of serene irony and even sadness, which puts it quite alone among [Dickens's] other works'.

As in the 1906 book so in these prefaces he frequently provides penetrating insights into central aspects of Dickens's work as when he is discussing his social criticism in the *Oliver Twist* essay:

> His revolt is not a revolt of the commercialist against the feudalist, of the Nonconformist against the Churchman, of the Free-trader against the Protectionist, of the Liberal against the Tory. . . . His revolt was simply and solely the eternal revolt; it was the revolt of the weak against the strong. He did not dislike this or that argument

for oppression; he disliked oppression. He disliked a certain look
on the face of a man when he looks down on another man.

This seems to me to go to the very heart of Dickens's
social attitudes and help us to understand what may often
seem confusing in his work – his shifting attitude towards
the French populace in *A Tale of Two Cities,* for example.

As Peter Hunt and others have shown, Chesterton antici-
pates in many places much later criticism of Dickens including
that of Edmund Wilson in his 1939 essay, 'Dickens: the
two Scrooges', often seen as the great foundation stone of
modern Dickens criticism. Chesterton's fine analysis of the
centripetal structure of *Bleak House* with its all-anticipating
first paragraphs is a good example. Similarly, when he
suggests that Dickens's novels are all 'outgrowths of the
original notion of taking notes, splendid and varied notes,
of what happens in the street' (p. 118) he looks forward to
Raymond Williams's famous observation that Dickens's way
of seeing his characters was essentially a street way of
seeing people. And, even when subsequent scholarship has
shown Chesterton to be wrong on a point of fact, e.g.,
with regard to Dickens's plans for *Our Mutual Friend* ('He
originally meant Boffin really to be corrupted by wealth'),
his actual critical point is often still perfectly valid: the
passage in which Boffin reveals that he has been only
pretending to be a miser *does* have 'something highly jerky
and unsatisfactory' about it. Moreover, this essay like the
others on the later novels shows us that, despite his much-
proclaimed preference for Dickens's earlier novels,
Chesterton was quite capable of writing very well about
the later ones, witness his acute and subtle discussion of
Richard Carstone in *Bleak House* as Dickens's only true
tragic hero.

Taken as a whole, Chesterton's *Criticisms and Appreciations* represents, by any standards, a major landmark in Dickens studies: they certainly deserve to be better known, less overshadowed by the 1906 book, splendid though that is. For, finally, whether or not Chesterton is, as many would argue, the greatest critic of Dickens there has ever been, he is certainly the most entertaining and the one who, by virtue of his temperament and his deepest beliefs about life and its meaning, is most profoundly in sympathy with his subject. As Patrick Braybrooke wrote in his *Dickensian* obituary in 1936:

> Chesterton had that love of humanity which was possessed by Dickens. He loved the ordinary man and the ordinary woman as did Dickens. He saw man made in the Image of God and he saw man, as did Dickens, often lost in a fog.

MICHAEL SLATER

Note: For further discussion of Chesterton on Dickens see the admirable special Dickens number of *The Chesterton Review,* vol. xi, no. 4 (November 1985), and 'Chesterton's use of Biography in his *Charles Dickens* (1906)' by Peter Hunt in *The Dickensian,* vol. 84 (Autumn 1988).

THE UNCOMMERCIAL TRAVELLER

The Uncommercial Traveller is a collection of Dickens's memories rather than of his literary purposes; but it is due to him to say that memory is often more startling in him than prophecy in anybody else. They have the character which belongs to all his vivid incidental writing: that they attach themselves always to some text which is a fact rather than an idea. He was one of those sons of Eve who are fonder of the Tree of Life than of the Tree of Knowledge—even of the knowledge of good and of evil. He was in this profoundest sense a realist. Critics have talked of an artist with his eye on the object. Dickens as an essayist always had his eye on an object before he had the faintest notion of a subject. All these works of his can best be considered as letters; they are notes of personal travel, scribbles in a diary about this or that that really happened. But Dickens was one of the few men who have the two talents that are the whole of literature—and have them both together. First, he could make a thing happen over again; and second, he could make it happen better. He can be called exaggerative; but mere exaggeration conveys nothing of his typical talent. Mere whirlwinds of words, mere melodramas of earth and heaven do not affect us as Dickens affects us, because they are exaggerations of nothing. If asked for an exaggeration of something, their inventors would be entirely dumb. They would not know how to exaggerate a broom-stick; for the life of them they could not exaggerate a tenpenny nail. Dickens always began with the nail or the broom-stick. He always began with a fact even when he was most fanciful; and even when he drew the long bow he was careful to hit the white.

This riotous realism of Dickens has its disadvantage —a disadvantage that comes out more clearly in these casual sketches than in his constructed romances. One grave defect in his greatness is that he was altogether too indifferent to theories. On large matters he went right by the very largeness of his mind; but in small matters he suffered from the lack of any logical test and ready reckoner. Hence his comment upon the details of civilisation or reform are sometimes apt to be jerky and jarring, and even grossly inconsistent. So long as a thing was heroic enough to admire, Dickens admired it; whenever it was absurd enough to laugh at he laughed at it: so far he was on sure ground. But about all the small human projects that lie between the extremes of the sublime and the ridiculous, his criticism was apt to have an accidental quality. As Matthew Arnold said of the remarks of the Young Man from the Country about the perambulator, they are felt not to be at the heart of the situation. On a great many occasions the Uncommercial Traveller seems, like other hasty travellers, to be criticising elements and institutions which he has quite inadequately understood; and once or twice the Uncommercial Traveller might almost as well be a Commercial Traveller for all he knows of the countryside.

An instance of what I mean may be found in the amusing article about the nightmares of the nursery. Superficially read it might almost be taken to mean that Dickens disapproved of ghost stories—disapproved of that old and genial horror which nurses can hardly supply fast enough for the children who want it. Dickens, one would have thought, should have been the last man in the world to object to horrible stories, having himself written some of the most horrible that exist in the world. The author of the Madman's Manuscript, of the disease of Monk and the death of Krook, cannot be considered fastidious in the matter of revolting realism or of revolting mysticism. If artistic horror is to be kept from the young, it is at least as necessary to keep little boys from reading *Pickwick* or *Bleak House* as to refrain from telling them the story of Captain Murderer or the terrible tale of Chips. If there was something appalling in the rhyme of Chips and pips and ships, it was nothing compared to that infernal refrain of "Mudstains, bloodstains" which Dickens himself, in one of his highest moments of hellish art, put into *Oliver Twist*.

I take this one instance of the excellent article called "Nurse's Stories" because it is quite typical of all the rest. Dickens (accused of superficiality by those who cannot grasp that there is foam upon deep seas) was really deep about human beings; that is, he was original and creative about them. But about ideas he did tend to be a little superficial. He judged them by whether they hit him, and not by what they were trying to hit.   Thus in this book the great wizard of the Christmas ghosts seems almost the enemy of ghost stories; thus the almost melodramatic moralist who created Ralph Nickleby and Jonas Chuzzlewit cannot see the point in original sin; thus the great denouncer of official oppression in England may be found far too indulgent to the basest aspects of the modern police.   His theories were less important than his creations, because he was a man of genius.   But he himself thought his theories the more important, because he was a man.

SKETCHES BY BOZ

THE greatest mystery about almost any great writer is why he was ever allowed to write at all. The first efforts of eminent men are always imitations; and very often they are bad imitations. The only question is whether the publisher had (as his name would seem to imply) some subconscious connection or sympathy with the public, and thus felt instinctively the presence of something that might ultimately tell; or whether the choice was merely a matter of chance and one Dickens was chosen and another Dickens left. The fact is almost unquestionable: most authors made their reputation by bad books and afterwards supported it by good ones. This is in some degree true even in the case of Dickens. The public continued to call him "Boz" long after the public had forgotten the *Sketches by Boz*. Numberless writers of the time speak of "Boz" as having written *Martin Chuzzlewit* and "Boz" as having written *David Copperfield*. Yet if they had gone back to the original book signed "Boz" they might even have felt that it was vulgar and flippant. This is indeed the chief tragedy of publishers: that they may easily refuse at the same moment the wrong manuscript and the right man. It is easy to see of Dickens now that he was the right man; but a man might have been very well excused if he had not realised that the *Sketches* was the right book.　Dickens, I say, is a case for this primary query: whether there was in the first work any clear sign of his higher creative spirit. But Dickens is much less a case for this query than almost all the other great men of his period.　The very earliest works of Thackeray are much more unimpressive than those of Dickens.　Nay, they are much more vulgar than those of Dickens.　And worst of all, they are much more numerous than those of Dickens.　Thackeray came much nearer to being the ordinary literary failure than Dickens ever came. Read some of the earliest criticisms of Mr. Yellowplush or Michael Angelo Titmarsh and you will realise that at the very beginning there was more potential clumsiness and silliness in Thackeray than there ever was in Dickens.　Nevertheless there was some potential clumsiness and silliness in Dickens; and what there is of it appears here and there in the admirable *Sketches by Boz*.

Perhaps we may put the matter this way: this is the only one of Dickens's works of which it is ordinarily necessary to know the date.　To a close and delicate comprehension it is indeed very important that *Nicholas Nickleby* was written at the beginning of Dickens's life, and *Our Mutual Friend* towards the end of it. Nevertheless anybody could understand or enjoy these books, whenever they were written.　If *Our Mutual Friend* was written in the Latin of the Dark Ages we should still want it translated.　If we thought that *Nicholas Nickleby* would not be written until thirty years hence we should all wait for it eagerly.　The general impression produced by Dickens's work is the same as that produced by miraculous visions; it is the destruction of time. Thomas Aquinas said that there was no time in the sight of God; however this may be, there was no time in the sight of Dickens. As a general rule Dickens can be read in any order; not only in any order of books, but even in any order of chapters. In an average Dickens book every part is so amusing and alive that you can read the parts backwards; you can read the quarrel first and then the cause of the quarrel; you can fall in love with a woman in the tenth chapter and then turn back to the first chapter to find out who she is. This is not chaos; it is eternity. It means merely that Dickens instinctively felt all his figures to be immortal souls who existed whether he wrote of them or not, and whether the reader read of them or not. There is a peculiar quality as of celestial pre-existence about the Dickens characters. Not only did they exist before we heard of them, they existed also before Dickens heard of them. As a rule this unchangeable air in Dickens deprives any discussion about date of its point. But as I have said, this is the one Dickens work of which the date *is* essential. It is really an important part of the criticism of this book to say that it is his first book. Certain elements of clumsiness, of obviousness, of evident blunder, actually require the chronological explanation. It is biographically important that this is his first book, almost exactly in the same way that it is biographically important that *The Mystery of Edwin Drood* was his last book. Change or no change, *Edwin Drood* has this plain point of a last story about it: that it is not finished. But if the last book is unfinished, the first book is more unfinished still.

The *Sketches* divide themselves, of course, into two broad classes. One half consists of sketches that are truly and in the strict sense sketches. That is, they are things that have no story and in their outline none of the character of creation; they are merely facts from the street or the tavern or the town hall, noted down as they occurred by an intelligence of quite exceptional vivacity. The second class consists of purely creative things: farces, romances, stories in any case with a non-natural perfection, or a poetical justice, to round them off. One class is admirably represented, for instance, by the sketch describing the Charity Dinner, the other by such a story as that of *Horatio Sparkins*. These things were almost certainly written by Dickens at very various periods of his youth; and early as the harvest is, no doubt it is a harvest and had ripened during a reasonably long time. Nevertheless it is with these two types of narrative that the young Charles Dickens first enters English literature; he enters it with a number of journalistic notes of such things as he has seen happen in streets or offices, and with a number of short stories which err on the side of the extravagant and even the superficial. Journalism had not then, indeed, sunk to the low level which it has since reached. His sketches of dirty London would not have been dirty enough for the modern Imperialist press. Still these first efforts of his are journalism, and sometimes vulgar journalism. It was as a journalist that he attacked the world, as a journalist that he conquered it.

The biographical circumstances will not, of course, be forgotten. The life of Dickens had been a curious one. Brought up in a family just poor enough to be painfully conscious of its prosperity and its respectability, he had been suddenly flung by a financial calamity into a social condition far below his own. For men on that exact edge of the educated class such a transition is really tragic. A duke may become a navvy for a joke, but a clerk cannot become a navvy for a joke. Dickens's parents went to a debtors' prison; Dickens himself went to a far more unpleasant place. The debtors' prison had about it at least that element of amiable compromise and kindly decay which belonged (and belongs still) to all the official institutions of England. But Dickens was doomed to see the very blackest aspect of nineteenth-century England, something far blacker than any mere bad government. He went not to a prison but to a factory. In the musty traditionalism of the Marshalsea old John Dickens could easily remain optimistic. In the ferocious efficiency of the modern factory young Charles Dickens narrowly escaped being a pessimist. He did escape this danger; finally he even escaped the factory itself. His next step in life was, if possible, even more eccentric. He was sent to school; he was sent off like an innocent little boy in Eton collars to learn the rudiments of Latin grammar, without any reference to the fact that he had already taken his part in the horrible competition and actuality of the age of manufactures. It was like giving a sacked bank manager a satchel and sending him to a dame's school. Nor was the third stage of this career unconnected with the oddity of the others. On leaving the school he was made a clerk in a lawyer's office, as if henceforward this child of ridiculous changes was to settle down into a silent assistant for a quiet solicitor. It was exactly at this moment that his fundamental rebellion began to seethe; it seethed more against the quiet finality of his legal occupation than it had seethed against the squalor and slavery of his days of poverty. There must have been in his mind, I think, a dim feeling: "Did all my dark crises mean only this; was I crucified only that I might become a solicitor's clerk?" Whatever be the truth about this conjecture there can be no question about the facts themselves. It was about this time that he began to burst and bubble over, to insist upon his own intellect, to claim a career. It was about this time that he put together a loose pile of papers, satires on institutions, pictures of private persons, fairy tales of the vulgarity of his world, odds and ends such as come out of the facility and the fierce vanity of youth. It was about this time at any rate that he decided to publish them, and gave them the name of *Sketches by Boz*.

They must, I think, be read in the light of this youthful explosion. In some psychological sense he had really been wronged. But he had only become conscious of his wrongs as his wrongs had been gradually righted. Similarly, it has often been found that a man who can patiently endure penal servitude through a judicial blunder will nevertheless, when once his cause is well asserted, quarrel about the amount of compensation or complain of small slights in his professional existence. These are the marks of the first literary action of Dickens. It has in it all the peculiar hardness of youth; a hardness which in those who have in any way been unfairly treated reaches even to impudence. It is a terrible thing for any man to find out that his elders are wrong. And this almost unkindly courage of youth must partly be held responsible for the smartness of Dickens, that almost offensive smartness which in these earlier books of his sometimes irritates us like the showy gibes in the tall talk of a school-boy. These first pages bear witness both to the energy of his genius and also to its unenlightenment; he seems more ignorant and more cocksure than so great a man should be. Dickens was never stupid, but he was sometimes silly; and he is occasionally silly here.

All this must be said to prepare the more fastidious modern for these papers, if he has never read them before. But when all this has been said there remains in them exactly what always remains in Dickens when you have taken away everything that can be taken away by the most fastidious modern who ever dissected his grandmother. There remains that *primum mobile* of which all the mystics have spoken: energy, the power to create. I will not call it "the will to live," for that is a priggish phrase of German professors. Even German professors, I suppose, have the will to live. But Dickens had exactly what German professors have not: he had the power to live. And indeed it is most valuable to have these early specimens of the Dickens work if only because they are specimens of his spirit apart from his matured intelligence. It is well to be able to realise that contact with the Dickens world is almost like a physical contact; it is like stepping suddenly into the hot smells of a greenhouse, or into the bleak smell of the sea. We know that we are there. Let any one read, for instance, one of the foolish but amusing farces in Dickens's first volume. Let him

read, for instance, such a story as that of *Horatio Sparkins*
or that of *The Tuggses at Ramsgate*. He will not find
very much of that verbal felicity or fantastic irony that
Dickens afterwards developed; the incidents are upon
the plain lines of the stock comedy of the day: sharpers
who entrap simpletons, spinsters who angle for husbands, youths who try to look Byronic and only look
foolish. Yet there is something in these stories which
there is not in the ordinary stock comedies of that
day: an indefinable flavour of emphasis and richness, a
hint as of infinity of fun. Doubtless, for instance, a
million comic writers of that epoch had made game of
the dark, romantic young man who pretended to abysses
of philosophy and despair. And it is not easy to say
exactly why we feel that the few metaphysical remarks
of Mr. Horatio Sparkins are in some way really much
funnier than any of those old stock jokes. It is in a
certain quality of deep enjoyment in the writer as well
as the reader; as if the few words written had been
dipped in dark nonsense and were, as it were, reeking
with derision. "Because if Effect be the result of
Cause and Cause be the Precursor of Effect," said Mr.
Horatio Sparkins, "I apprehend that you are wrong."
Nobody can get at the real secret of sentences like that;
sentences which were afterwards strewed with reckless
liberality over the conversation of Dick Swiveller or
Mr. Mantalini, Sim Tappertit or Mr. Pecksniff.
Though the joke seems most superficial one has only
to read it a certain number of times to see that it is
most subtle. The joke does not lie in Mr. Sparkins
merely using long words, any more than the joke lies
merely in Mr. Swiveller drinking, or in Mr. Mantalini

deceiving his wife. It is something in the arrangement of the words; something in a last inspired turn of absurdity given to a sentence. In spite of everything Horatio Sparkins is funny. We cannot tell why he is funny. When we know why he is funny we shall know why Dickens is great.

Standing as we do here upon the threshold, as it were, of the work of Dickens, it may be well perhaps to state this truth as being, after all, the most important one. This first work had, as I have said, the faults of first work and the special faults that arose from its author's accidental history; he was deprived of education, and therefore it was in some ways uneducated; he was confronted with the folly and failure of his natural superiors and guardians, and therefore it was in some ways pert and insolent. Nevertheless the main fact about the work is worth stating here for any reader who should follow the chronological order and read the *Sketches by Boz* before embarking on the stormy and splendid sea of *Pickwick*. For the sea of *Pickwick*, though splendid, does make some people seasick. The great point to be emphasised at such an initiation is this: that people, especially refined people, are not to judge of Dickens by what they would call the coarseness or commonplaceness of his subject. It is quite true that his jokes are often on the same *subjects* as the jokes in a halfpenny comic paper. Only they happen to be good jokes. He does make jokes about drunkenness, jokes about mothers-in-law, jokes about henpecked husbands, jokes (which is much more really unpardonable) about spinsters, jokes about physical cowardice, jokes about fatness, jokes about sitting down on one's hat. He does make fun of all these things; and the reason is not very far to seek. He makes fun of all these things because all these things, or nearly all of them, are really very funny. But a large number of those who might otherwise read and enjoy Dickens are undoubtedly "put off" (as the phrase goes) by the fact that he seems to be echoing a poor kind of claptrap in his choice of incidents and images. Partly, of course, he suffers from the very fact of his success; his play with these topics was so good that every one else has played with them increasingly since; he may indeed have copied the old jokes, but he certainly renewed them. For instance, "Ally Sloper" was certainly copied from Wilkins Micawber. To this day you may see (in the front page of that fine periodical) the bald head and the high shirt collar that betray the high original from which "Ally Sloper" is derived. But exactly because "Sloper" was stolen from Micawber, for that very reason the new generation feels as if Micawber were stolen from "Sloper." Many modern readers feel as if Dickens were copying the comic papers, whereas in truth the comic papers are still copying Dickens.

Dickens showed himself to be an original man by always accepting old and established topics. There is no clearer sign of the absence of originality among modern poets than their disposition to find new themes. Really original poets write poems about the spring. They are always fresh, just as the spring is always fresh. Men wholly without originality write poems about torture, or new religions, of some perversion of obscenity, hoping that the mere sting of the subject may speak for them. But we do not sufficiently realise

that what is true of the classic ode is also true of the
classic joke. A true poet writes about the spring being
beautiful because (after a thousand springs) the spring
really is beautiful. In the same way the true humourist
writes about a man sitting down on his hat, because the
act of sitting down on one's hat (however often and
however admirably performed) really is extremely
funny. We must not dismiss a new poet because his
poem is called *To a Skylark;* nor must we dismiss a
humourist because his new farce is called *My Mother-in-
law.* He may really have splendid and inspiring things
to say upon an eternal problem. The whole question
is whether he has.

Now this is exactly where Dickens, and the possible
mistake about Dickens, both come in. Numbers of
sensitive ladies, numbers of simple æsthetes, have had a
vague shrinking from that element in Dickens which
begins vaguely in *The Tuggses at Ramsgate* and culminates in *Pickwick.* They have a vague shrinking from
the mere subject matter; from the mere fact that so
much of the fun is about drinking or fighting, or falling
down, or eloping with old ladies. It is to these that
the first appeal must be made upon the threshold of
Dickens criticism. Let them really read the thing
and really see whether the humour is the gross and half-
witted jeering which they imagine it to be. It is
exactly here that the whole genius of Dickens is concerned. His subjects are indeed stock subjects; like
the skylark of Shelley, or the autumn of Keats. But
all the more because they are stock subjects the reader
realises what a magician is at work. The notion of a
clumsy fellow who falls off his horse is indeed a stock

and stale subject.   But Mr. Winkle is not a stock and
stale subject.   Nor is his horse a stock and stale subject;
it is as immortal as the horses of Achilles.   The notion
of a fat old gentleman proud of his legs might easily
be vulgar.   But Mr. Pickwick proud of his legs is not
vulgar; somehow we feel that they were legs to be
proud of.   And it is exactly this that we must look for
in these *Sketches*.   We must not leap to any cheap
fancy that they are low farces.   Rather we must see
that they are not low farces; and see that nobody but
Dickens could have prevented them from being so.

PICKWICK PAPERS

THERE are those who deny with enthusiasm the existence of a God and are happy in a hobby which they call the Mistakes of Moses. I have not studied their labours in detail, but it seems that the chief mistake of Moses was that he neglected to write the Pentateuch. The lesser errors, apparently, were not made by Moses, but by another person equally unknown. These controversialists cover the very widest field, and their attacks upon Scripture are varied to the point of wildness. They range from the proposition that the unexpurgated Bible is almost as unfit for an American girls' school as is an unexpurgated Shakespeare; they descend to the proposition that kissing the Book is almost as hygienically dangerous as kissing the babies of the poor. A superficial critic might well imagine that there was not one single sentence left of the Hebrew or Christian Scriptures which this school had not marked with some ingenious and uneducated comment. But there is one passage at least upon which they have never pounced, at least to my knowledge; and in pointing it out to them I feel that I am, or ought to be, providing material for quite a multitude of Hyde Park orations. I mean that singular arrangement in the mystical account of the Creation by which light is created first and all the luminous bodies afterwards. One could not imagine a process more open to the elephantine logic of the Bible-smasher than this: that the sun should be created after the sunlight. The conception that lies at the back of the phrase is indeed profoundly antagonistic to much of the modern point of view. To many modern people it would sound like saying that foliage existed before the first leaf; it would sound like saying that childhood existed before a baby was born. The idea is, as I have said, alien to most modern thought, and like many other ideas which are alien to most modern thought, it is a very subtle and a very sound idea. Whatever be the meaning of the passage in the actual primeval poem, there is a very real metaphysical meaning in the idea that light existed before the sun and stars. It is not barbaric; it is rather Platonic. The idea existed before any of the machinery which made manifest the idea. Justice existed when there was no need of judges, and mercy existed before any man was oppressed.

However this may be in the matter of religion and philosophy, it can be said with little exaggeration that this truth is the very key of literature. The whole difference between construction and creation is exactly this: that a thing constructed can only be loved after it is constructed; but a thing created is loved before it exists, as the mother can love the unborn child. In creative art the essence of a book exists before the book or before even the details or main features of the book; the author enjoys it and lives in it with a kind of prophetic rapture. He wishes to write a comic story before he has thought of a single comic incident. He desires to write a sad story before he has thought of anything sad. He knows the atmosphere before he knows anything. There is a low priggish maxim sometimes uttered by men so frivolous as to take humour seriously—a maxim that a man should not laugh at his own jokes. But the great artist not only laughs at his own jokes; he laughs at his own jokes before he has made them. In the case of a man really humorous we can see humour in his eye before he has thought of any amusing words at all. So the creative writer laughs at his comedy before he creates it, and he has tears for his tragedy before he knows what it is. When the symbols and the fulfilling facts do come to him, they come generally in a manner very fragmentary and inverted, mostly in irrational glimpses of crisis or consummation. The last page comes before the first; before his romance has begun, he knows that it has ended well. He sees the wedding before the wooing; he sees the death before the duel. But most of all he sees the colour and character of the whole story prior to any possible events in it. This is the real argument for art and style, only that the artists and the stylists have not the sense to use it. In one very real sense style is far more important than either character or narrative. For a man knows what style of book he wants to write when he knows nothing else about it.

Pickwick is in Dickens's career the mere mass of light before the creation of sun or moon. It is the splendid, shapeless substance of which all his stars were ultimately made. You might split up *Pickwick* into innumerable novels as you could split up that primeval light into innumerable solar systems. The *Pickwick Papers* constitute first and foremost a kind of wild promise, a pre-natal vision of all the children of Dickens. He had not yet settled down into the plain, professional habit of picking out a plot and characters, of attending to one thing at a time, of writing a separate, sensible novel and sending it off to his publishers. He is still in the youthful whirl of the kind of world that he would like to create. He has not yet really settled what story he will write, but only what sort of story he will write. He tries to tell ten stories at once; he pours into the pot all the chaotic fancies and crude experiences of his boyhood; he sticks in irrelevant short stories shamelessly, as into a scrap-book; he adopts designs and abandons them, begins episodes and leaves them unfinished; but from the first page to the last there is a nameless and elemental ecstasy—that of the man who is doing the kind of thing that he can do. Dickens, like every other honest and effective writer, came at last to some degree of care and self-restraint. He learned how to make his *dramatis personæ* assist his drama; he learned how to write stories which were full of rambling and perversity, but which were stories. But before he wrote a single real story, he had a kind of vision. It was a vision of the Dickens world—a maze of white roads, a map full of fantastic towns, thundering coaches, clamorous market-places, uproarious inns, strange and swaggering figures. That vision was *Pickwick*.

It must be remembered that this is true even in connection with the man's contemporaneous biography. Apart from anything else about it, *Pickwick* was his first great chance. It was a big commission given in some sense to an untried man, that he might show what he could do. It was in a strict sense a sample. And just as a sample of leather can be only a piece of leather, or a sample of coal a lump of coal, so this book may most properly be regarded as simply a lump of Dickens. He was anxious to show all that was in him. He was more concerned to prove that he could write well than to prove that he could write this particular book well. And he did prove this, at any rate. No one ever sent such a sample as the sample of Dickens. His roll of leather blocked up the street; his lump of coal set the Thames on fire.

The book originated in the suggestion of a publisher; as many more good books have done than the arrogance of the man of letters is commonly inclined to admit. Very much is said in our time about Apollo and Admetus, and the impossibility of asking genius to work within prescribed limits or assist an alien design. But after all, as a matter of fact, some of the greatest geniuses have done it, from Shakespeare botching up bad comedies and dramatising bad novels down to Dickens writing a masterpiece as the mere framework for a Mr. Seymour's sketches. Nor is the true explanation irrelevant to the spirit and power of Dickens. Very delicate, slender, and *bizarre* talents are indeed incapable of being used for an outside purpose, whether of public good or of private gain. But about very great and rich talent there goes a certain disdainful generosity which can turn its hand to anything. Minor poets cannot write to order; but very great poets can write to order. The larger the man's mind, the wider his scope of vision, the more likely it will be that anything suggested to him will seem significant and promising; the more he has a grasp of everything the more ready he will be to write anything. It is very hard (if that is the question) to throw a brick at a man and ask him to write an epic; but the more he is a great man the more able he will be to write about the brick. It is very unjust (if that is all) to point to a hoarding of Colman's mustard and demand a flood of philosophical eloquence; but the greater the man is the more likely he will be to give it to you. So it was proved, not for the first time, in this great experiment of the early employment of Dickens. Messrs. Chapman and Hall came to him with a scheme for a string of sporting stories to serve as the context, and one might almost say the excuse, for a string of sketches by Seymour, the sporting artist. Dickens made some modifications in the plan, but he adopted its main feature; and its main feature was Mr. Winkle. To think of what Mr. Winkle might have been in the hands of a dull *farceur*, and then to think of what he is, is to experience the feeling that Dickens made a man out of rags and refuse. Dickens was to work splendidly and successfully in many fields, and to send forth many brilliant books and brave figures. He was destined to have the applause of continents like a statesman, and to dictate to his publishers like a despot; but perhaps he never worked again so supremely well as here, where he worked in chains. It may well be questioned whether his one hack book is not his masterpiece.

Of course it is true that as he went on his independence increased, and he kicked quite free of the influences that had suggested his story. So Shakespeare declared his independence of the original chronicle of Hamlet, Prince of Denmark, eliminating altogether (with some wisdom) another uncle called Wiglerus. At the start the Nimrod Club of Chapman and Hall may have even had equal chances with the Pickwick Club of young Mr. Dickens; but the Pickwick Club became something much better than any publisher had dared to dream of. Some of the old links were indeed severed by accident or extraneous trouble; Seymour, for whose sake the whole had perhaps been planned, blew his brains out before he had drawn ten pictures. But such things were trifles compared to *Pickwick* itself. It mattered little now whether Seymour blew his brains out, so long as Charles Dickens blew his brains in. The work became systematically and progressively more powerful and masterly. Many critics have commented on the somewhat discordant and inartistic change between the earlier part of *Pickwick* and the later; they have pointed out, not without good sense, that the character of Mr. Pickwick changes from that of a silly buffoon to that of a solid merchant. But the case, if these critics had noticed it, is much stronger in the minor characters of the great company. Mr. Winkle, who has been an idiot (even, perhaps, as Mr. Pickwick says, "an impostor"), suddenly becomes a romantic and even reckless lover, scaling a forbidden wall and planning a bold elopement. Mr. Snodgrass, who has behaved in a ridiculous manner in all serious positions, suddenly finds himself in a ridiculous position —that of a gentleman surprised in a secret love affair— and behaves in a manner perfectly manly, serious, and honourable. Mr. Tupman alone has no serious emotional development, and for this reason it is, presumably, that we hear less and less of Mr. Tupman towards the end of the book. Dickens has by this time got into a thoroughly serious mood—a mood expressed indeed by extravagant incidents, but none the less serious for that; and into this Winkle and Snodgrass, in the character of romantic lovers, could be made to fit. Mr. Tupman had to be left out of the love affairs; therefore Mr. Tupman is left out of the book.

Much of the change was due to the entrance of the greatest character in the story. It may seem strange at the first glance to say that Sam Weller helped to make the story serious. Nevertheless, this is strictly true. The introduction of Sam Weller had, to begin with, some merely accidental and superficial effects. When Samuel Weller had appeared, Samuel Pickwick was no longer the chief farcical character. Weller became the joker and Pickwick in some sense the butt of his jokes. Thus it was obvious that the more simple, solemn, and really respectable this butt could be made the better. Mr. Pickwick had been the figure capering before the footlights. But with the advent of Sam, Mr. Pickwick had become a sort of black background and had to behave as such. But this explanation, though true as far as it goes, is a mean and unsatisfactory one, leaving the great elements unexplained. For a much deeper and more righteous reason Sam Weller introduces the more serious tone of Pickwick. He introduces it because he introduces something which it was the chief business of Dickens to preach throughout his life—something which he never preached so well as when he preached it unconsciously. Sam Weller introduces the English people.

Sam Weller is the great symbol in English literature of the populace peculiar to England. His incessant stream of sane nonsense is a wonderful achievement of Dickens: but it is no great falsification of the incessant stream of sane nonsense as it really exists among the English poor. The English poor live in an atmosphere of humour; they think in humour. Irony is the very air that they breathe. A joke comes suddenly from time to time into the head of a politician or a gentleman, and then as a rule he makes the most of it; but when a serious word comes into the mind of a coster it is almost as startling as a joke. The word "chaff" was, I suppose, originally applied to badinage to express its barren and unsustaining character; but to the English poor chaff is as sustaining as grain. The phrase that leaps to their lips is the ironical phrase. I remember once being driven in a hansom cab down a street that turned out to be a *cul de sac*, and brought us bang up against a wall. The driver and I simultaneously said something. But I said: "This 'll never do!" and he said: "This is all right!" Even in the act of pulling back his horse's nose from a brick wall, that confirmed satirist thought in terms of his highly-trained and traditional satire; while I, belonging to a duller and simpler class, expressed my feelings in words as innocent and literal as those of a rustic or a child.

This eternal output of divine derision has never been so truly typified as by the character of Sam; he is a grotesque fountain which gushes the living waters for ever. Dickens is accused of exaggeration and he is often guilty of exaggeration; but here he does not exaggerate: he merely symbolises and sublimates like any other great artist. Sam Weller does not exaggerate the wit of the London street arab one atom more than Colonel Newcome, let us say, exaggerates the stateliness of an ordinary soldier and gentleman, or than Mr. Collins exaggerates the fatuity of a certain kind of country clergyman. And this breath from the boisterous brotherhood of the poor lent a special seriousness and smell of reality to the whole story. The unconscious follies of Winkle and Tupman are blown away like leaves before the solid and conscious folly of Sam Weller. Moreover, the relations between Pickwick and his servant Sam are in some ways new and valuable in literature. Many comic writers had described the clever rascal and his ridiculous dupe; but here, in a fresh and very human atmosphere, we have a clever servant who was not a rascal and a dupe and who was not ridiculous. Sam Weller stands in some ways for a cheerful knowledge of the world; Mr. Pickwick stands for a still more cheerful ignorance of the world. And Dickens responded to a profound human sentiment (the sentiment that has made saints and the sanctity of children) when he made the gentler and less-travelled type—the type which moderates and controls. Knowledge and innocence are both excellent things, and they are both very funny. But it is right that knowledge should be the servant and innocence the master.

The sincerity of this study of Sam Weller has produced one particular effect in the book which I wonder that critics of Dickens have never noticed or discussed. Because it has no Dickens "pathos," certain parts of it are truly pathetic. Dickens, realising rightly that the whole tone of the book was fun, felt that he ought to keep out of it any great experiments in sadness and keep within limits those that he put in. He used this restraint in order not to spoil the humour; but (if he had known himself better) he might well have used it in order not to spoil the pathos. This is the one book in which Dickens was, as it were, forced to trample down his tender feelings; and for that very reason it is the one book where all the tenderness there is is quite unquestionably true. An admirable example of what I mean may be found in the scene in which Sam Weller goes down to see his bereaved father after the death of his step-mother. The most loyal admirer of Dickens can hardly prevent himself from giving a slight shudder when he thinks of what Dickens might have made of that scene in some of his more expansive and maudlin moments. For all I know old Mrs. Weller might have asked what the wild waves were saying; and for all I know old Mr. Weller might have told her. As it is, Dickens, being forced to keep the tale taut and humorous, gives a picture of humble respect and decency which is manly, dignified, and really sad. There is no attempt made by these simple and honest men, the father and son, to pretend that the dead woman was anything greatly other than she was; their respect is for death, and for the human weakness and mystery which it must finally cover. Old Tony Weller does not tell his shrewish wife that she is already a white-winged angel; he speaks to her with an admirable good nature and good sense:

"'Susan,' I says, 'you've been a wery good vife to me altogether: keep a good heart, my dear, and you 'll live to see me punch that 'ere Stiggins's 'ead yet.' She smiled at this, Samivel . . . but she died arter all."

That is perhaps the first and the last time that Dickens ever touched the extreme dignity of pathos. He is restraining his compassion, and afterwards he let it go. Now laughter is a thing that can be let go; laughter has in it a quality of liberty. But sorrow has in it by its very nature a quality of confinement; pathos by its very nature fights with itself. Humour is expansive; it bursts outwards; the fact is attested by the common expression, "holding one's sides." But sorrow is not expansive; and it was afterwards the mistake of Dickens that he tried to make it expansive. It is the one great weakness of Dickens as a great writer, that he did try to make that sudden sadness, that abrupt pity, which we call pathos, a thing quite obvious, infectious, public, as if it were journalism or the measles. It is pleasant to think that in this supreme masterpiece, done in the dawn of his career, there is not even this faint fleck upon the sun of his just splendour. Pickwick will always be remembered as the great example of everything that made Dickens great; of the solemn conviviality of great friendships, of the erratic adventures of old English roads, of the hospitality of old English inns, of the great fundamental kindliness and honour of old English manners. First of all, however, it will always be remembered for its laughter, or, if you will, for its folly. A good joke is the one ultimate and sacred thing which

cannot be criticised. Our relations with a good joke
are direct and even divine relations. We speak of
"seeing" a joke just as we speak of "seeing" a ghost or
a vision. If we have seen it, it is futile to argue with
us; and we have seen the vision of *Pickwick*. *Pickwick* may be the top of Dickens's humour; I think upon
the whole it is. But the broad humour of *Pickwick* he
broadened over many wonderful kingdoms; the narrow
pathos of *Pickwick* he never found again.

NICHOLAS NICKLEBY

ROMANCE is perhaps the highest point of human expression, except indeed religion, to which it is closely allied. Romance resembles religion especially in this, that it is not only a simplification but a shortening of existence. Both romance and religion see everything as it were foreshortened; they see everything in an abrupt and fantastic perspective, coming to an apex. It is the whole essence of perspective that it comes to a point. Similarly, religion comes to a point—to the point. Thus religion is always insisting on the shortness of human life. But it does not insist on the shortness of human life as the pessimists insist on it. Pessimism insists on the shortness of human life in order to show that life is valueless. Religion insists on the shortness of human life in order to show that life is frightfully valuable—is almost horribly valuable. Pessimism says that life is so short that it gives nobody a chance; religion says that life is so short that it gives everybody his final chance. In the first case the word brevity means futility; in the second case, opportunity. But the case is even stronger than this. Religion shortens everything. Religion shortens even eternity. Where science, submitting to the false standard of time, sees evolution, which is slow, religion sees creation, which is sudden. Philosophically speaking, the process is neither slow nor quick since we have nothing to compare it with. Religion prefers to think of it as quick. For religion the flowers shoot up suddenly like rockets. For religion the mountains are lifted up suddenly like waves. Those who quote that fine passage which says that in God's sight a thousand years are as yesterday that is passed as a watch in the night, do not realise the full force of the meaning. To God a thousand years are not only a watch but an exciting watch. For God time goes at a gallop, as it does to a man reading a good tale.

All this is, in a humble manner, true for romance. Romance is a shortening and sharpening of the human difficulty. Where you and I have to vote against a man, or write (rather feebly) against a man, or sign illegible petitions against a man, romance does for him what we should really like to see done. It knocks him down; it shortens the slow process of historical justice. All romances consist of three characters. Other characters may be introduced; but those other characters are certainly mere scenery as far as the romance is concerned. They are bushes that wave rather excitedly; they are posts that stand up with a certain pride; they are correctly painted rocks that frown very correctly; but they are all landscape—they are all a background. In every pure romance there are three living and moving characters. For the sake of argument they may be called St. George and the Dragon and the Princess. In every romance there must be the twin elements of loving and fighting. In every romance there must be the three characters: there must be the Princess, who is a thing to be loved; there must be the Dragon, who is a thing to be fought; and there must be St. George, who is a thing that both loves and fights. There have been many symptoms of cynicism and decay in our modern civilisation. But of all the signs of modern feebleness, of lack of grasp on morals as they actually must be, there has been none quite so silly or so dangerous as this: that the philosophers of to-day have started to divide loving from fighting and to put them into opposite camps. There could be no worse sign than that a man, even Nietzsche, can be found to say that we should go in for fighting instead of loving. There can be no worse sign than that a man, even Tolstoi, can be found to tell us that we should go in for loving instead of fighting. The two things imply each other; they implied each other in the old romance and in the old religion, which were the two permanent things of humanity. You cannot love a thing without wanting to fight for it. You cannot fight without something to fight for. To love a thing without wishing to fight for it is not love at all; it is lust. It may be an airy, philosophical, and disinterested lust; it may be, so to speak, a virgin lust; but it is lust, because it is wholly self-indulgent and invites no attack. On the other hand, fighting for a thing without loving it is not even fighting; it can only be called a kind of horse-play that is occasionally fatal. Wherever human nature is human and unspoilt by any special sophistry, there exists this natural kinship between war and wooing, and that natural kinship is called romance. It comes upon a man especially in the great hour of youth; and every man who has ever been young at all has felt, if only for a moment, this ultimate and poetic paradox. He knows that loving the world is the same thing as fighting the world. It was at the very moment when he offered to like everybody he also offered to hit everybody. To almost every man that can be called a man this especial moment of the romantic culmination has come. In the first resort the man wished to live a romance. In the second resort, in the last and worst resort, he was content to write one.

Now there is a certain moment when this element enters independently into the life of Dickens. There is a particular time when we can see him suddenly realise that he wants to write a romance and nothing else. In reading his letters, in appreciating his character, this point emerges clearly enough. He was full of the afterglow of his marriage; he was still young and psychologically ignorant; above all, he was now, really for the first time, sure that he was going to be at least some kind of success. There is, I repeat, a certain point at which one feels that Dickens will either begin to write romances or go off on something different altogether. This crucial point in his life is marked by *Nicholas Nickleby*.

It must be remembered that before this issue of *Nicholas Nickleby* his work, successful as it was, had not been such as to dedicate him seriously or irrevocably to the writing of novels. He had already written three books; and at least two of them are classed among the novels under his name. But if we look at the actual origin and formation of these books we see that they came from another source and were really designed upon another plan. The three books were, of course, the *Sketches by Boz*, the *Pickwick Papers*, and *Oliver Twist*.

It is, I suppose, sufficiently well understood that the *Sketches by Boz* are, as their name implies, only sketches. But surely it is quite equally clear that the *Pickwick Papers* are, as their name implies, merely papers. Nor is the case at all different in spirit and essence when we come to *Oliver Twist*. There is indeed a sort of romance in *Oliver Twist*, but it is such an uncommonly bad one that it can hardly be regarded as greatly interrupting the previous process; and if the reader chooses to pay very little attention to it, he cannot pay less attention to it than the author did. But in fact the case lies far deeper. *Oliver Twist* is so much apart from the ordinary track of Dickens, it is so gloomy, it is so much all in one atmosphere, that it can best be considered as an exception or a solitary excursus in his work. Perhaps it can best be considered as the extension of one of his old sketches, of some sketch that happened to be about a visit to a workhouse or a gaol. In the *Sketches by Boz* he might well have visited a workhouse where he saw Bumble; in the *Sketches by Boz* he might well have visited a prison where he saw Fagin. We are still in the realm of sketches and sketchiness. The *Pickwick Papers* may be called an extension of one of his bright sketches. *Oliver Twist* may be called an extension of one of his gloomy ones.

Had he continued along this line all his books might very well have been note-books. It would be very easy to split up all his subsequent books into scraps and episodes, such as those which make up the *Sketches by Boz*. It would be easy enough for Dickens, instead of publishing *Nicholas Nickleby*, to have published a book of sketches, one of which was called "A Yorkshire

School," another called "A Provincial Theatre," and another called "Sir Mulberry Hawk or High Life Revealed," another called " Mrs. Nickleby or a Lady's Monologue." It would have been very easy to have thrown over the rather chaotic plan of the *Old Curiosity Shop*. He might have merely written short stories called " The Glorious Apollos," " Mrs. Quilp's Tea-Party," " Mrs. Jarley's Waxwork," " The Little Servant," and " The Death of a Dwarf." *Martin Chuzzlewit* might have been twenty stories instead of one story. *Dombey and Son* might have been twenty stories instead of one story. We might have lost all Dickens's novels; we might have lost altogether Dickens the novelist. We might have lost that steady love of a seminal and growing romance which grew on him steadily as the years advanced, and which gave us towards the end some of his greatest triumphs. All his books might have been *Sketches by Boz*. But he did turn away from this, and the turning-point is *Nicholas Nickleby*.

Everything has a supreme moment and is crucial; that is where our friends the evolutionists go wrong. I suppose that there is an instant of midsummer as there is an instant of midnight. If in the same way there is a supreme point of spring, *Nicholas Nickleby* is the supreme point of Dickens's spring. I do not mean that it is the best book that he wrote in his youth. *Pickwick* is a better book. I do not mean that it contains more striking characters than any of the other books in his youth. The *Old Curiosity Shop* contains at least two more striking characters. But I mean that this book coincided with his resolution to be a great novelist and his final belief that he could be one.

Henceforward his books are novels, very commonly
bad novels. Previously they have not really been
novels at all. There are many indications of the change
I mean. Here is one, for instance, which is more or
less final. *Nicholas Nickleby* is Dickens's first romantic
novel because it is his first novel with a proper and
dignified romantic hero; which means, of course, a
somewhat chivalrous young donkey. The hero of
Pickwick is an old man. The hero of *Oliver Twist* is a
child. Even after *Nicholas Nickleby* this non-romantic
custom continued. The *Old Curiosity Shop* has no
hero in particular. The hero of *Barnaby Rudge* is a
lunatic. But Nicholas Nickleby is a proper, formal,
and ceremonial hero. He has no psychology; he has
not even any particular character; but he is made
deliberately a hero—young, poor, brave, unimpeachable, and ultimately triumphant. He is, in short, the
hero. Mr. Vincent Crummles had a colossal intellect;
and I always have a fancy that under all his pomposity
he saw things more keenly than he allowed others to
see. The moment he saw Nicholas Nickleby, almost
in rags and limping along the high road, he engaged
him (you will remember) as first walking gentleman.
He was right. Nobody could possibly be more of a
first walking gentleman than Nicholas Nickleby was.
He was the first walking gentleman before he went on
to the boards of Mr. Vincent Crummles's theatre, and
he remained the first walking gentleman after he had
come off.

Now this romantic method involves a certain element
of climax which to us appears crudity. Nicholas
Nickleby, for instance, wanders through the world; he

takes a situation as assistant to a Yorkshire school-master; he sees an act of tyranny of which he strongly disapproves; he cries out "Stop!" in a voice that makes the rafters ring; he thrashes the schoolmaster within an inch of his life; he throws the schoolmaster away like an old cigar, and he goes away. The modern intellect is positively prostrated and flattened by this rapid and romantic way of righting wrongs. If a modern philanthropist came to Dotheboys Hall I fear he would not employ the simple, sacred, and truly Christian solution of beating Mr. Squeers with a stick. I fancy he would petition the Government to appoint a Royal Commission to inquire into Mr. Squeers. I think he would every now and then write letters to newspapers reminding people that, in spite of all appearances to the contrary, there was a Royal Com-mission to inquire into Mr. Squeers. I agree that he might even go the length of calling a crowded meeting in St. James's Hall on the subject of the best policy with regard to Mr. Squeers. At this meeting some very heated and daring speakers might even go the length of alluding sternly to Mr. Squeers. Occasionally even hoarse voices from the back of the hall might ask (in vain) what was going to be done with Mr. Squeers. The Royal Commission would report about three years afterwards and would say that many things had hap-pened which were certainly most regrettable; that Mr. Squeers was the victim of a bad system; that Mrs. Squeers was also the victim of a bad system; but that the man who sold Squeers his cane had really acted with great indiscretion and ought to be spoken to kindly. Something like this would be what, after four years, the Royal Commission would have said; but it would not matter in the least what the Royal Commission had said, for by that time the philanthropists would be off on a new tack and the world would have forgotten all about Dotheboys Hall and everything connected with it. By that time the philanthropists would be petitioning Parliament for another Royal Commission; perhaps a Royal Commission to inquire into whether Mr. Mantalini was extravagant with his wife's money; perhaps a commission to inquire into whether Mr. Vincent Crummles kept the Infant Phenomenon short by means of gin.

If we wish to understand the spirit and the period of *Nicholas Nickleby* we must endeavour to comprehend and to appreciate the old more decisive remedies, or, if we prefer to put it so, the old more desperate remedies. Our fathers had a plain sort of pity; if you will, a gross and coarse pity. They had their own sort of sentimentalism. They were quite willing to weep over Smike. But it certainly never occurred to them to weep over Squeers. Even those who opposed the French war opposed it exactly in the same way as their enemies opposed the French soldiers. They fought with fighting. Charles Fox was full of horror at the bitterness and the useless bloodshed; but if any one had insulted him over the matter, he would have gone out and shot him in a duel as coolly as any of his contemporaries. All their interference was heroic interference. All their legislation was heroic legislation. All their remedies were heroic remedies. No doubt they were often narrow and often visionary. No doubt they often looked at a political formula when they should have looked at an elemental fact. No doubt they were pedantic in some of their principles and clumsy in some of their solutions. No doubt, in short, they were all very wrong; and no doubt we are the people, and wisdom shall die with us. But when they saw something which in their eyes, such as they were, really violated their morality, such as it was, then they did not cry "Investigate!" They did not cry "Educate!" They did not cry "Improve!" They did not cry "Evolve!" Like Nicholas Nickleby they cried "Stop!" And it did stop.

This is the first mark of the purely romantic method: the swiftness and simplicity with which St. George kills the dragon. The second mark of it is exhibited here as one of the weaknesses of *Nicholas Nickleby*. I mean the tendency in the purely romantic story to regard the heroine merely as something to be won; to regard the princess solely as something to be saved from the dragon. The father of Madeline Bray is really a very respectable dragon. His selfishness is suggested with much more psychological tact and truth than that of any other of the villains that Dickens described about this time. But his daughter is merely the young woman with whom Nicholas is in love. We do not care a rap about Madeline Bray. Personally I should have preferred Cecilia Bobster. Here is one real point where the Victorian romance falls below the Elizabethan romantic drama. Shakespeare always made his heroines heroic as well as his heroes.

In Dickens's actual literary career it is this romantic quality in *Nicholas Nickleby* that is most important. It is his first definite attempt to write a young and chivalrous novel. In this sense the comic characters and the comic scenes are secondary; and indeed the comic characters and the comic scenes, admirable as they are, could never be considered as in themselves superior to such characters and such scenes in many of the other books. But in themselves how unforgettable they are. Mr. Crummles and the whole of his theatrical business is an admirable case of that first and most splendid quality in Dickens—I mean the art of making something which in life we call pompous and dull, becoming in literature pompous and delightful. I have remarked before that nearly every one of the amusing characters of Dickens is in reality a great fool. But I might go further. Almost every one of his amusing characters is in reality a great bore. The very people that we fly to in Dickens are the very people that we fly from in life. And there is more in Crummles than the mere entertainment of his solemnity and his tedium. The enormous seriousness with which he takes his art is always an exact touch in regard to the unsuccessful artist. If an artist is successful, everything then depends upon a dilemma of his moral character. If he is a mean artist success will make him a society man. If he is a magnanimous artist, success will make him an ordinary man. But only as long as he is unsuccessful will he be an unfathomable and serious artist, like Mr. Crummles. Dickens was always particularly good at expressing thus the treasures that belong to those who do not succeed in this world. There are vast prospects and splendid songs in the point of view of the typically unsuccessful man; if all the used-up actors and spoilt journalists and broken clerks could give a chorus, it would be a wonderful chorus in praise of the world. But these unsuccessful men commonly cannot even speak. Dickens is the voice of them, and a very ringing voice; because he was perhaps the only one of these unsuccessful men that was ever successful.

OLIVER TWIST

In considering Dickens, as we almost always must consider him, as a man of rich originality, we may possibly miss the forces from which he drew even his original energy. It is not well for man to be alone. We, in the modern world, are ready enough to admit that when it is applied to some problem of monasticism or of an ecstatic life. But we will not admit that our modern artistic claim to absolute originality is really a claim to absolute unsociability; a claim to absolute loneliness. The anarchist is at least as solitary as the ascetic. And the men of very vivid vigour in literature, the men such as Dickens, have generally displayed a large sociability towards the society of letters, always expressed in the happy pursuit of pre-existent themes, sometimes expressed, as in the case of Molière or Sterne, in downright plagiarism. For even theft is a confession of our dependence on society. In Dickens, however, this element of the original foundations on which he worked is quite especially difficult to determine. This is partly due to the fact that for the present reading public he is practically the only one of his long line that is read at all. He sums up Smollett and Goldsmith, but he also destroys them. This one giant, being closest to us, cuts off from our view even the

giants that begat him.   But much more is this difficulty
due to the fact that Dickens mixed up with the old
material, materials so subtly modern, so made of the
French Revolution, that the whole is transformed.
If we want the best example of this, the best example
is *Oliver Twist*.

Relatively to the other works of Dickens *Oliver
Twist* is not of great value, but it is of great importance.   Some parts of it are so crude and of so clumsy
a melodrama, that one is almost tempted to say that
Dickens would have been greater without it.   But
even if he had been greater without it he would still
have been incomplete without it.   With the exception
of some gorgeous passages, both of humour and horror,
the interest of the book lies not so much in its revelation
of Dickens's literary genius as in its revelation of those
moral, personal, and political instincts which were the
make-up of his character and the permanent support of
that literary genius.   It is by far the most depressing
of all his books; it is in some ways the most irritating;
yet its ugliness gives the last touch of honesty to all
that spontaneous and splendid output.   Without this
one discordant note all his merriment might have
seemed like levity.

Dickens had just appeared upon the stage and set
the whole world laughing with his first great story
Pickwick. *Oliver Twist* was his encore.   It was the
second opportunity given to him by those who had
rolled about with laughter over Tupman and Jingle,
Weller and Dowler. Under such circumstances a
stagey reciter will sometimes take care to give a pathetic
piece after his humorous one; and with all his many

moral merits, there was much that was stagey about
Dickens. But this explanation alone is altogether
inadequate and unworthy. There was in Dickens
this other kind of energy, horrible, uncanny, barbaric,
capable in another age of coarseness, greedy for the
emblems of established ugliness, the coffin, the gibbet,
the bones, the bloody knife. Dickens liked these things
and he was all the more of a man for liking them;
especially he was all the more of a boy. We can all
recall with pleasure the fact that Miss Petowker
(afterwards Mrs. Lillyvick) was in the habit of reciting
a poem called "The Blood Drinker's Burial." I cannot
express my regret that the words of this poem are not
given; for Dickens would have been quite as capable
of writing "The Blood Drinker's Burial" as Miss Petowker was of reciting it. This strain existed in Dickens
alongside of his happy laughter; both were allied to the
same robust romance. Here as elsewhere Dickens is
close to all the permanent human things. He is close
to religion, which has never allowed the thousand
devils on its churches to stop the dancing of its bells.
He is allied to the people, to the real poor, who love
nothing so much as to take a cheerful glass and to talk
about funerals. The extremes of his gloom and gaiety
are the mark of religion and democracy; they mark
him off from the moderate happiness of philosophers,
and from that stoicism which is the virtue and the creed
of aristocrats. There is nothing odd in the fact that
the same man who conceived the humane hospitalities
of Pickwick should also have imagined the inhuman
laughter of Fagin's den. They are both genuine and
they are both exaggerated. And the whole human

tradition has tied up together in a strange knot these strands of festivity and fear. It is over the cups of Christmas Eve that men have always competed in telling ghost stories.

This first element was present in Dickens, and it is very powerfully present in *Oliver Twist*. It had not been present with sufficient consistency or continuity in *Pickwick* to make it remain on the reader's memory at all, for the tale of "Gabriel Grubb" is grotesque rather than horrible, and the two gloomy stories of the "Madman" and the "Queer Client" are so utterly irrelevant to the tale, that even if the reader remember them he probably does not remember that they occur in *Pickwick*. Critics have complained of Shakespeare and others for putting comic episodes into a tragedy. It required a man with the courage and coarseness of Dickens actually to put tragic episodes into a farce. But they are not caught up into the story at all. In *Oliver Twist*, however, the thing broke out with an almost brutal inspiration, and those who had fallen in love with Dickens for his generous buffoonery may very likely have been startled at receiving such very different fare at the next helping. When you have bought a man's book because you like his writing about Mr. Wardle's punch-bowl and Mr. Winkle's skates, it may very well be surprising to open it and read about the sickening thuds that beat out the life of Nancy, or that mysterious villain whose face was blasted with disease.

As a nightmare, the work is really admirable. Characters which are not very clearly conceived as regards their own psychology are yet, at certain moments, managed so as to shake to its foundations our own psychology. Bill Sikes is not exactly a real man, but for all that he is a real murderer. Nancy is not really impressive as a living woman; but (as the phrase goes) she makes a lovely corpse. Something quite childish and eternal in us, something which is shocked with the mere simplicity of death, quivers when we read of those repeated blows or see Sikes cursing the tell-tale cur who will follow his bloody foot-prints. And this strange, sublime, vulgar melodrama, which is melodrama and yet is painfully real, reaches its hideous height in that fine scene of the death of Sikes, the besieged house, the boy screaming within, the crowd screaming without, the murderer turned almost a maniac and dragging his victim uselessly up and down the room, the escape over the roof, the rope swiftly running taut, and death sudden, startling and symbolic; a man hanged. There is in this and similar scenes something of the quality of Hogarth and many other English moralists of the early eighteenth century. It is not easy to define this Hogarthian quality in words, beyond saying that it is a sort of alphabetical realism, like the cruel candour of children. But it has about it these two special principles which separate it from all that we call realism in our time. First, that with us a moral story means a story about moral people; with them a moral story meant more often a story about immoral people. Second, that with us realism is always associated with some subtle view of morals; with them realism was always associated with some simple view of morals. The end of Bill Sikes exactly in the way that the law would have killed him—this is a Hogarthian incident; it

carries on that tradition of startling and shocking
platitude.

All this element in the book was a sincere thing in the
author, but none the less it came from old soils, from
the graveyard and the gallows, and the lane where the
ghost walked. Dickens was always attracted to such
things, and (as Forster says with inimitable simplicity)
"but for his strong sense might have fallen into the
follies of spiritualism." As a matter of fact, like most
of the men of strong sense in his tradition, Dickens was
left with a half belief in spirits which became in practice
a belief in bad spirits. The great disadvantage of
those who have too much strong sense to believe in
supernaturalism is that they keep last the low and little
forms of the supernatural, such as omens, curses,
spectres, and retributions, but find a high and happy
supernaturalism quite incredible. Thus the Puritans
denied the sacraments, but went on burning witches.
This shadow does rest, to some extent, upon the rational English writers like Dickens; supernaturalism
was dying, but its ugliest roots died last. Dickens
would have found it easier to believe in a ghost than in
a vision of the Virgin with angels. There, for good or
evil, however, was the root of the old *diablerie* in
Dickens, and there it is in *Oliver Twist*. But this was
only the first of the new Dickens elements, which
must have surprised those Dickensians who eagerly
bought his second book. The second of the new
Dickens elements is equally indisputable and separate.
It swelled afterwards to enormous proportions in
Dickens's work; but it really has its rise here. Again,
as in the case of the element of *diablerie*, it would be

possible to make technical exceptions in favour of
Pickwick. Just as there were quite inappropriate
scraps of the gruesome element in *Pickwick*, so there
are quite inappropriate allusions to this other topic
in *Pickwick*. But nobody by merely reading *Pickwick*
would even remember this topic; no one by merely
reading *Pickwick* would know what this topic is; this
third great subject of Dickens; this second great subject of the Dickens of *Oliver Twist*.

This subject is social oppression. It is surely fair to
say that no one could have gathered from *Pickwick*
how this question boiled in the blood of the author of
Pickwick. There are, indeed, passages, particularly
in connection with Mr. Pickwick in the debtor's
prison, which prove to us, looking back on a whole
public career, that Dickens had been from the beginning
bitter and inquisitive about the problem of our civilisation. No one could have imagined at the time that
this bitterness ran in an unbroken river under all the
surges of that superb gaiety and exuberance. With
Oliver Twist this sterner side of Dickens was suddenly
revealed. For the very first pages of *Oliver Twist* are
stern even when they are funny. They amuse, but
they cannot be enjoyed, as can the passages about the
follies of Mr. Snodgrass or the humiliations of Mr.
Winkle. The difference between the old easy humour
and this new harsh humour is a difference not of degree
but of kind. Dickens makes game of Mr. Bumble
because he wants to kill Mr. Bumble; he made game of
Mr. Winkle because he wanted him to live for ever.
Dickens has taken the sword in hand; against what is
he declaring war?

It is just here that the greatness of Dickens comes in; it is just here that the difference lies between the pedant and the poet. Dickens enters the social and political war, and the first stroke he deals is not only significant but even startling. Fully to see this we must appreciate the national situation. It was an age of reform, and even of radical reform; the world was full of radicals and reformers; but only too many of them took the line of attacking everything and anything that was opposed to some particular theory among the many political theories that possessed the end of the eighteenth century. Some had so much perfected the perfect theory of republicanism that they almost lay awake at night because Queen Victoria had a crown on her head. Others were so certain that mankind had hitherto been merely strangled in the bonds of the State that they saw truth only in the destruction of tariffs or of by-laws. The greater part of that generation held that clearness, economy, and a hard common-sense, would soon destroy the errors that had been erected by the superstitions and sentimentalities of the past. In pursuance of this idea many of the new men of the new century, quite confident that they were invigorating the new age, sought to destroy the old sentimental clericalism, the old sentimental feudalism, the old-world belief in priests, the old-world belief in patrons, and among other things the old-world belief in beggars. They sought among other things to clear away the old visionary kindliness on the subject of vagrants. Hence those reformers enacted not only a new reform bill but also a new poor law. In creating many other modern things they created the modern workhouse, and when Dickens came out to fight it was the first thing that he broke with his battle-axe.

This is where Dickens's social revolt is of more value than mere politics and avoids the vulgarity of the novel with a purpose. His revolt is not a revolt of the commercialist against the feudalist, of the Nonconformist against the Churchman, of the Free-trader against the Protectionist, of the Liberal against the Tory. If he were among us now his revolt would not be the revolt of the Socialist against the Individualist, or of the Anarchist against the Socialist. His revolt was simply and solely the eternal revolt; it was the revolt of the weak against the strong. He did not dislike this or that argument for oppression; he disliked oppression. He disliked a certain look on the face of a man when he looks down on another man. And that look on the face is, indeed, the only thing in the world that we have really to fight between here and the fires of Hell. That which pedants of that time and this time would have called the sentimentalism of Dickens was really simply the detached sanity of Dickens. He cared nothing for the fugitive explanations of the Constitutional Conservatives; he cared nothing for the fugitive explanations of the Manchester School. He would have cared quite as little for the fugitive explanations of the Fabian Society or of the modern scientific Socialist. He saw that under many forms there was one fact, the tyranny of man over man; and he struck at it when he saw it, whether it was old or new. When he found that footmen and rustics were too much afraid of Sir Leicester Dedlock, he attacked Sir Leicester Dedlock; he did not care whether Sir Leicester Dedlock said he was attacking England or whether Mr. Rouncewell, the Ironmaster, said he was attacking an effete oligarchy. In that case he pleased Mr. Rouncewell, the Ironmaster, and displeased Sir Leicester Dedlock, the Aristocrat. But when he found that Mr. Rouncewell's workmen were much too frightened of Mr. Rouncewell, then he displeased Mr. Rouncewell in turn; he displeased Mr. Rouncewell very much by calling him Mr. Bounderby. When he imagined himself to be fighting old laws he gave a sort of vague and general approval to new laws. But when he came to the new laws they had a bad time. When Dickens found that after a hundred economic arguments and granting a hundred economic considerations, the fact remained that paupers in modern workhouses were much too afraid of the beadle, just as vassals in ancient castles were much too afraid of the Dedlocks, then he struck suddenly and at once. This is what makes the opening chapters of *Oliver Twist* so curious and important. The very fact of Dickens's distance from, and independence of, the elaborate financial arguments of his time, makes more definite and dazzling his sudden assertion that he sees the old human tyranny in front of him as plain as the sun at noon-day. Dickens attacks the modern workhouse with a sort of inspired simplicity as of a boy in a fairy tale who had wandered about, sword in hand, looking for ogres and who had found an indisputable ogre. All the other people of his time are attacking things because they are bad economics or because they are bad politics, or because they are bad science; he alone is attacking things because they are bad. All the others are Radicals with a large R; he

alone is radical with a small one. He encounters evil
with that beautiful surprise which, as it is the beginning
of all real pleasure, is also the beginning of all righteous
indignation. He enters the workhouse just as Oliver
Twist enters it, as a little child.

This is the real power and pathos of that celebrated
passage in the book which has passed into a proverb;
but which has not lost its terrible humour even in being
hackneyed. I mean, of course, the everlasting quotation about Oliver Twist asking for more. The real
poignancy that there is in this idea is a very good study
in that strong school of social criticism which Dickens
represented. A modern realist describing the dreary
workhouse would have made all the children utterly
crushed, not daring to speak at all, not expecting anything, not hoping anything, past all possibility of
affording even an ironical contrast or a protest of despair. A modern, in short, would have made all the
boys in the workhouse pathetic by making them all
pessimists. But Oliver Twist is not pathetic because
he is a pessimist. Oliver Twist is pathetic because he is
an optimist. The whole tragedy of that incident is in
the fact that he does expect the universe to be kind to
him, that he does believe that he is living in a just
world. He comes before the Guardians as the ragged
peasants of the French Revolution came before the
Kings and Parliaments of Europe. That is to say,
he comes, indeed, with gloomy experiences, but he
comes with a happy philosophy. He knows that there
are wrongs of man to be reviled; but he believes also
that there are rights of man to be demanded. It has
often been remarked as a singular fact that the French

poor, who stand in historic tradition as typical of all
the desperate men who have dragged down tyranny,
were, as a matter of fact, by no means worse off than the
poor of many other European countries before the Revolution. The truth is that the French were tragic
because they were better off. The others had known
the sorrowful experiences; but they alone had known
the splendid expectation and the original claims. It
was just here that Dickens was so true a child of them
and of that happy theory so bitterly applied. They
were the one oppressed people that simply asked for
justice; they were the one Parish Boy who innocently
asked for more.

OLD CURIOSITY SHOP

NOTHING is important except the fate of the soul; and literature is only redeemed from an utter triviality, surpassing that of naughts and crosses, by the fact that it describes not the world around us or the things on the retina of the eye or the enormous irrelevancy of encyclopædias, but some condition to which the human spirit can come. All good writers express the state of their souls, even (as occurs in some cases of very good writers) if it is a state of damnation. The first thing that has to be realised about Dickens is this ultimate spiritual condition of the man, which lay behind all his creations. This Dickens state of mind is difficult to pick out in words as are all elementary states of mind; they cannot be described, not because they are too subtle for words, but because they are too simple for words. Perhaps the nearest approach to a statement of it would be this: that Dickens expresses an eager anticipation of everything that will happen in the motley affairs of men; he looks at the quiet crowd waiting for it to be picturesque and to play the fool; he expects everything; he is torn with a happy hunger. Thackeray is always looking back to yesterday; Dickens is always looking forward to to-morrow. Both are profoundly humorous, for there is a humour of the morning and a humour of the evening; but the first guesses at what it will get, at all the grotesqueness and variety which a day may bring forth; the second looks back on what the day has been and sees even its solemnities as slightly ironical. Nothing can be too extravagant for the laughter that looks forward; and nothing can be too dignified for the laughter that looks back. It is an idle but obvious thing, which many must have noticed, that we often find in the title of one of an author's books what might very well stand for a general description of all of them. Thus all Spenser's works might be called *A Hymn to Heavenly Beauty;* or all Mr. Bernard Shaw's bound books might be called *You Never Can Tell.* In the same way the whole substance and spirit of Thackeray might be gathered under the general title *Vanity Fair.* In the same way too the whole substance and spirit of Dickens might be gathered under the general title *Great Expectations.*

In a recent criticism on this position I saw it remarked that all this is reading into Dickens something that he did not mean; and I have been told that it would have greatly surprised Dickens to be informed that he "went down the broad road of the Revolution." Of course it would. Criticism does not exist to say about authors the things that they knew themselves. It exists to say the things about them which they did not know themselves. If a critic says that the *Iliad* has a pagan rather than a Christian pity, or that it is full of pictures made by one epithet, of course he does not mean that Homer could have said that. If Homer could have said that the critic would leave Homer to say it. The function of criticism, if it has a legitimate function at all, can only be one function—

that of dealing with the subconscious part of the author's mind which only the critic can express, and not with the conscious part of the author's mind, which the author himself can express. Either criticism is no good at all (a very defensible position) or else criticism means saying about an author the very things that would have made him jump out of his boots.

Doubtless the name in this case *Great Expectations* is an empty coincidence; and indeed it is not in the books of the later Dickens period (the period of *Great Expectations*) that we should look for the best examples of this sanguine and expectant spirit which is the essential of the man's genius. There are plenty of good examples of it especially in the earlier works. But even in the earlier works there is no example of it more striking or more satisfactory than *The Old Curiosity Shop*. It is particularly noticeable in the fact that its opening and original framework express the idea of a random experience, a thing come across in the street; a single face in the crowd, followed until it tells its story. Though the thing ends in a novel it begins in a sketch; it begins as one of the *Sketches by Boz*. There is something unconsciously artistic in the very clumsiness of this opening. Master Humphrey starts to keep a scrap-book of all his adventures, and he finds that he can fill the whole scrap-book with the sequels and developments of one adventure; he goes out to notice everybody and he finds himself busily and variedly occupied only in watching somebody. In this there is a very profound truth about the true excitement and inexhaustible poetry of life. The truth is not so much that eternity is full of souls as that one soul can

fill eternity. In strict art there is something quite
lame and lumbering about the way in which the benevolent old story-teller starts to tell many stories and
then drops away altogether, while one of his stories
takes his place. But in a larger art, his collision with
Little Nell and his complete eclipse by her personality
and narrative have a real significance. They suggest
the random richness of such meetings, and their un-
calculated results. It makes the whole book a sort of
splendid accident.

It is not true, as is commonly said, that the Dickens
pathos as pathos is bad. It is not true, as is still more
commonly said, that the whole business about Little
Nell is bad. The case is more complex than that.
Yet complex as it is it admits of one sufficiently clear
distinction. Those who have written about the death
of Little Nell, have generally noticed the crudities of
the character itself; the little girl's unnatural and
staring innocence, her constrained and awkward piety.
But they have nearly all of them entirely failed to
notice that there is in the death of Little Nell one
quite definite and really artistic idea. It is not an
artistic idea that a little child should die rhetorically on
the stage like Paul Dombey; and Little Nell does not
die rhetorically upon the stage like Paul Dombey. But
it is an artistic idea that all the good powers and personalities in the story should set out in pursuit of one
insignificant child, to repair an injustice to her, should
track her from town to town over England with all the
resources of wealth, intelligence, and travel, and should
all—arrive too late. All the good fairies and all the
kind magicians, all the just kings and all the gallant

princes, with chariots and flying dragons and armies and navies go after one little child who had strayed into a wood, and find her dead. That is the conception which Dickens's artistic instinct was really aiming at when he finally condemned Little Nell to death, after keeping her, so to speak, so long with the rope round her neck. The death of Little Nell is open certainly to the particular denial which its enemies make about it. The death of Little Nell is not pathetic. It is perhaps tragic; it is in reality ironic. Here is a very good case of the injustice to Dickens on his purely literary side. It is not that I say that Dickens achieved what he designed; it is that the critics will not see what the design was. They go on talking of the death of Little Nell as if it were a mere example of maudlin description like the death of Little Paul. As a fact it is not described at all; so it cannot be objectionable. It is not the death of Little Nell, but the life of Little Nell, that I object to.

In this, in the actual picture of her personality, if you can call it a personality, Dickens did fall into some of his facile vices. The real objection to much of his pathos belongs really to another part of his character. It is connected with his vanity, his voracity for all kinds of praise, his restive experimentalism and even perhaps his envy. He strained himself to achieve pathos. His humour was inspiration; but his pathos was ambition. His laughter was lonely; he would have laughed on a desert island. But his grief was gregarious. He liked to move great masses of men, to melt them into tenderness, to play on the people as a great pianist plays on them; to make them mad or sad. His pathos

was to him a way of showing his power; and for that
reason it was really powerless. He could not help making people laugh; but he tried to make them cry. We
come in this novel, as we often do come in his novels,
upon hard lumps of unreality, upon a phrase that suddenly sickens. That is always due to his conscious
despotism over the delicate feelings; that is always due
to his love of fame as distinct from his love of fun. But
it is not true that all Dickens's pathos is like this; it is
not even true that all the passages about Little Nell are
like this; there are two strands almost everywhere and
they can be differentiated as the sincere and the deliberate. There is a great difference between Dickens
thinking about the tears of his characters and Dickens
thinking about the tears of his audience.

When all this is allowed, however, and the exaggerated contempt for the Dickens pathos is properly
corrected, the broad fact remains: that to pass from
the solemn characters in this book to the comic characters in this book, is to be like some Ulysses who should
pass suddenly from the land of shadows to the mount-
ain of the gods. Little Nell has her own position in
careful and reasonable criticism: even that wobbling old
ass, her grandfather, has his position in it; perhaps even
the dissipated Fred (whom long acquaintance with
Mr. Dick Swiveller has not made any less dismal in
his dissipation) has a place in it also. But when we
come to Swiveller and Sampson Brass and Quilp and
Mrs. Jarley, then Fred and Nell and the grandfather
simply do not exist. There are no such people in the
story. The real hero and heroine of *The Old Curiosity
Shop* are of course Dick Swiveller and the Marchioness.

It is significant in a sense that these two sane, strong, living, and lovable human beings are the only two, or almost the only two, people in the story who do not run after Little Nell. They have something better to do than to go on that shadowy chase after that cheerless phantom. They have to build up between them a true romance; perhaps the one true romance in the whole of Dickens. Dick Swiveller really has all the half-heroic characteristics which make a man respected by a woman and which are the male contribution to virtue. He is brave, magnanimous, sincere about himself, amusing, absurdly hopeful; above all, he is both strong and weak. On the other hand the Marchioness really has all the characteristics, the entirely heroic characteristics which make a woman respected by a man. She is female: that is, she is at once incurably candid and incurably loyal, she is full of terrible common-sense, she expects little pleasure for herself and yet she can enjoy bursts of it; above all, she is physically timid and yet she can face anything. All this solid rocky romanticism is really implied in the speech and action of these two characters and can be felt behind them all the time. Because they are the two most absurd people in the book they are also the most vivid, human, and imaginable. There are two really fine love affairs in Dickens; and I almost think only two. One is the happy courtship of Swiveller and the Marchioness; the other is the tragic courtship of Toots and Florence Dombey. When Dick Swiveller wakes up in bed and sees the Marchioness playing cribbage he thinks that he and she are a prince and princess in a fairy tale. He thinks right.

I speak thus seriously of such characters with a deliberate purpose; for the frivolous characters of Dickens are taken much too frivolously. It has been quite insufficiently pointed out that all the serious moral ideas that Dickens did contrive to express he expressed altogether through this fantastic medium, in such figures as Swiveller and the little servant. The warmest upholder of Dickens would not go to the solemn or sentimental passages for anything fresh or suggestive in faith or philosophy. No one would pretend that the death of little Dombey (with its "What are the wild waves saying?") told us anything new or real about death. A good Christian dying, one would imagine, not only would not know what the wild waves were saying, but would not care. No one would pretend that the repentance of old Paul Dombey throws any light on the pyschology or philosophy of repentance. No doubt old Dombey, white-haired and amiable, was a great improvement on old Dombey brown-haired and unpleasant. But in his case the softening of the heart seems to bear too close a resemblance to softening of the brain. Whether these serious passages are as bad as the critical people or as good as the sentimental people find them, at least they do not convey anything in the way of an illuminating glimpse or a bold suggestion about men's moral nature. The serious figures do not tell one anything about the human soul. The comic figures do. Take anything almost at random out of these admirable speeches of Dick Swiveller. Notice, for instance, how exquisitely Dickens has caught a certain very deep and delicate quality at the bottom of this idle kind of man. I mean that odd impersonal sort of intellectual justice, by which the frivolous fellow sees things as they are and even himself as he is; and is above irritation.   Mr. Swiveller, you remember, asks the Marchioness whether the Brass family ever talk about him; she nods her head with vivacity. " 'Complimentary?' inquired Mr. Swiveller.   The motion of the little servant's head altered. . . . 'But she says,' continued the little servant, 'that you ain't to be trusted.'   'Well, do you know, Marchioness,' said Mr. Swiveller thoughtfully, 'many people, not exactly professional people, but tradesmen, have had the same idea.   The excellent citizen from whom I ordered this beer inclines strongly to that opinion.' "

This philosophical freedom from all resentment, this strange love of truth which seems actually to come through carelessness, is a very real piece of spiritual observation.   Even among liars there are two classes, one immeasurably better than another.   The honest liar is the man who tells the truth about his old lies; who says on Wednesday, "I told a magnificent lie on Monday."   He keeps the truth in circulation; no one version of things stagnates in him and becomes an evil secret.   He does not have to live with old lies; a horrible domesticity.   Mr. Swiveller may mislead the waiter about whether he has the money to pay; but he does not mislead his friend, and he does not mislead himself on the point.   He is quite as well aware as any one can be of the accumulating falsity of the position of a gentleman who by his various debts has closed up all the streets into the Strand except one, and who is going to close that to-night with a pair of gloves.

He shuts up the street with a pair of gloves, but he does not shut up his mind with a secret. The traffic of truth is still kept open through his soul.

It is exactly in these absurd characters, then, that we can find a mass of psychological and ethical suggestion. This cannot be found in the serious characters except indeed in some of the later experiments: there is a little of such psychological and ethical suggestion in figures like Gridley, like Jasper, like Bradley Headstone. But in these earlier books at least, such as *The Old Curiosity Shop*, the grave or moral figures throw no light upon morals. I should maintain this generalisation even in the presence of that apparent exception *The Christmas Carol* with its trio of didactic ghosts. Charity is certainly splendid, at once a luxury and a necessity; but Dickens is not most effective when he is preaching charity seriously; he is most effective when he is preaching it uproariously; when he is preaching it by means of massive personalities and vivid scenes. One might say that he is best not when he is preaching his human love, but when he is practising it. In his grave pages he tells us to love men; but in his wild pages he creates men whom we can love. By his solemnity he commands us to love our neighbours. By his caricature he makes us love them.

There is an odd literary question which I wonder is not put more often in literature. How far can an author tell a truth without seeing it himself? Perhaps an actual example will express my meaning. I was once talking to a highly intelligent lady about Thackeray's *Newcomes*. We were speaking of the character of Mrs. Mackenzie, the Campaigner, and in the middle of the conversation the lady leaned across to me and said in a low, hoarse, but emphatic voice, "She drank. Thackeray did n't know it; but she drank." And it is really astonishing what a shaft of white light this sheds on the Campaigner, on her terrible temperament, on her agonised abusiveness and her almost more agonised urbanity, on her clamour which is nevertheless not open or explicable, on her temper which is not so much bad temper as insatiable, bloodthirsty, man-eating temper. How far can a writer thus indicate by accident a truth of which he is himself ignorant? If truth is a plan or pattern of things that really are, or in other words, if truth truly exists outside ourselves, or in other words, if truth exists at all, it must be often possible for a writer to uncover a corner of it which he happens not to understand, but which his reader does happen to understand. The author sees only two lines; the reader sees where they meet and what is the angle. The author sees only an arc or fragment of a curve; the reader sees the size of the circle. The last thing to say about Dickens, and especially about books like *The Old Curiosity Shop*, is that they are full of these unconscious truths. The careless reader may miss them. The careless author almost certainly did miss them. But from them can be gathered an impression of real truth to life which is for the grave critics of Dickens an almost unknown benefit, buried treasure. Here for instance is one of them out of *The Old Curiosity Shop*. I mean the passage in which (by a blazing stroke of genius) the dashing Mr. Chuckster, one of the Glorious Apollos of whom Mr. Swiveller was the Perpetual Grand, is made to entertain a hatred bordering upon frenzy

for the stolid, patient, respectful, and laborious Kit.
Now in the formal plan of the story Mr. Chuckster is
a fool, and Kit is almost a hero; at least he is a noble
boy. Yet unconsciously Dickens made the idiot
Chuckster say something profoundly suggestive on the
subject. In speaking of Kit Mr. Chuckster makes use
of these two remarkable phrases; that Kit is "meek"
and that he is "a snob." Now Kit is really a very fresh
and manly picture of a boy, firm, sane, chivalrous, reasonable, full of those three great Roman virtues which Mr.
Belloc has so often celebrated, *virtus* and *verecundia* and
pietas. He is a sympathetic but still a straightforward
study of the best type of that most respectable of all
human classes, the respectable poor. All this is true;
all that Dickens utters in praise of Kit is true; nevertheless the awful words of Chuckster remain written on
the eternal skies. Kit is meek and Kit is a snob. His
natural dignity does include and is partly marred by
that instinctive subservience to the employing class
which has been the comfortable weakness of the whole
English democracy, which has prevented their making
any revolution for the last two hundred years. Kit
would not serve any wicked man for money, but
he would serve any moderately good man and the
money would give a certain dignity and decisiveness to
the goodness. All this is the English popular evil which
goes along with the English popular virtues of geniality,
of homeliness, tolerance and strong humour, hope and
an enormous appetite for a hand-to-mouth happiness.
The scene in which Kit takes his family to the theatre
is a monument of the massive qualities of old English
enjoyment. If what we want is Merry England, our

antiquarians ought not to revive the Maypole or the Morris Dancers; they ought to revive Astley's and Sadler's Wells and the old solemn Circus and the old stupid Pantomime, and all the sawdust and all the oranges. Of all this strength and joy in the poor, Kit is a splendid and final symbol. But amid all his masculine and English virtue, he has this weak touch of meekness, or acceptance of the powers that be. It is a sound touch; it is a real truth about Kit. But Dickens did not know it. Mr. Chuckster did.

Dickens's stories taken as a whole have more artistic unity than appears at the first glance. It is the immediate impulse of a modern critic to dismiss them as mere disorderly scrap-books with very brilliant scraps. But this is not quite so true as it looks. In one of Dickens's novels there is generally no particular unity of construction; but there is often a considerable unity of sentiment and atmosphere. Things are irrelevant, but not somehow inappropriate. The whole book is written carelessly; but the whole book is generally written in one mood. To take a rude parallel from the other arts, we may say that there is not much unity of form, but there is much unity of colour. In most of the novels this can be seen. *Nicholas Nickleby*, as I have remarked, is full of a certain freshness, a certain light and open-air curiosity, which irradiates from the image of the young man swinging along the Yorkshire roads in the sun. Hence the comic characters with whom he falls in are comic characters in the same key; they are a band of strolling players, charlatans and poseurs, but too humane to be called humbugs. In the same way, the central story of

Oliver Twist is sombre; and hence even its comic character is almost sombre; at least he is too ugly to be merely amusing. Mr. Bumble is in some ways a terrible grotesque; his apoplectic visage recalls the "fire-red Cherubimme's face," which added such horror to the height and stature of Chaucer's Sompnour. In both these cases even the riotous and absurd characters are a little touched with the tint of the whole story. But this neglected merit of Dickens can certainly be seen best in *The Old Curiosity Shop*.

The curiosity shop itself was a lumber of grotesque and sinister things, outlandish weapons, twisted and diabolic decorations. The comic characters in the book are all like images bought in an old curiosity shop. Quilp might be a gargoyle. He might be some sort of devilish door-knocker, dropped down and crawling about the pavement. The same applies to the sinister and really terrifying stiffness of Sally Brass. She is like some old staring figure cut out of wood. Sampson Brass, her brother, again is a grotesque in the same rather inhuman manner; he is especially himself when he comes in with the green shade over his eye. About all this group of bad figures in *The Old Curiosity Shop* there is a sort of *diablerie*. There is also within this atmosphere an extraordinary energy of irony and laughter. The scene in which Sampson Brass draws up the description of Quilp, supposing him to be dead, reaches a point of fiendish fun. "We will not say very bandy, Mrs. Jiniwin," he says of his friend's legs, "we will confine ourselves to bandy. He is gone, my friends, where his legs would never be called in question." They go on to the discussion of his nose, and

Mrs. Jiniwin inclines to the view that it is flat. "Aquiline, you hag! Aquiline," cries Mr. Quilp, pushing in his head and striking his nose with his fist. There is nothing better in the whole brutal exuberance of the character than that gesture with which Quilp punches his own face with his own fist. It is indeed a perfect symbol; for Quilp is always fighting himself for want of anybody else. He is energy, and energy by itself is always suicidal; he is that primordial energy which tears and which destroys itself.

BARNABY RUDGE

Barnaby Rudge was written by Dickens in the spring
and first flowing tide of his popularity; it came immediately after *The Old Curiosity Shop*, and only a
short time after *Pickwick*. Dickens was one of those
rare but often very sincere men in whom the high
moment of success almost coincides with the high moment of youth. The calls upon him at this time
were insistent and overwhelming; this necessarily
happens at a certain stage of a successful writer's
career. He was just successful enough to invite offers
and not successful enough to reject them. At the
beginning of his career he could throw himself into
Pickwick because there was nothing else to throw himself into. At the end of his life he could throw himself
into *A Tale of Two Cities*, because he refused to throw
himself into anything else. But there was an inter-
vening period, early in his life, when there was almost
too much work for his imagination, and yet not quite
enough work for his housekeeping. To this period
Barnaby Rudge belongs. And it is a curious tribute
to the quite curious greatness of Dickens that in this
period of youthful strain we do not feel the strain but
feel only the youth. His own amazing wish to write
equalled or outstripped even his readers' amazing
wish to read. Working too hard did not cure him of

his abstract love of work. Unreasonable publishers
asked him to write ten novels at once; but he wanted
to write twenty novels at once. All this period is
strangely full of his own sense at once of fertility and
of futility; he did work which no one else could have
done, and yet he could not be certain as yet that he
was anybody.

Barnaby Rudge marks this epoch because it marks
the fact that he is still confused about what kind of
person he is going to be. He has already struck the
note of the normal romance in *Nicholas Nickleby;* he
has already created some of his highest comic characters
in *Pickwick* and *The Old Curiosity Shop*, but here he
betrays the fact that it is still a question what ultimate
guide he shall follow. *Barnaby Rudge* is a romantic,
historical novel. Its design reminds us of Scott;
some parts of its fulfilment remind us, alas! of Harri-
son Ainsworth. It is a very fine romantic historical
novel; Scott would have been proud of it. But it is
still so far different from the general work of Dickens
that it is permissible to wonder how far Dickens was
proud of it. The book, effective as it is, is almost
entirely devoted to dealings with a certain artistic
element, which (in its mere isolation) Dickens did not
commonly affect; an element which many men of
infinitely less genius have often seemed to affect more
successfully; I mean the element of the picturesque.

It is the custom in many quarters to speak somewhat
sneeringly of that element which is broadly called the
picturesque. It is always felt to be an inferior, a
vulgar, and even an artificial form of art. Yet two
things may be remarked about it. The first is that,

with few exceptions, the greatest literary artists have been not only particularly clever at the picturesque, but particularly fond of it. Shakespeare, for instance, delighted in certain merely pictorial contrasts which are quite distinct from, even when they are akin to, the spiritual view involved. For instance, there is admirable satire in the idea of Touchstone teaching worldly wisdom and worldly honour to the woodland yokels. There is excellent philosophy in the idea of the fool being the representative of civilisation in the forest. But quite apart from this deeper meaning in the incident, the mere figure of the jester, in his bright motley and his cap and bells, against the green background of the forest and the rude forms of the shepherds, is a strong example of the purely picturesque. There is excellent tragic irony in the confrontation of the melancholy philosopher among the tombs with the cheerful digger of the graves. It sums up the essential point, that dead bodies can be comic; it is only dead souls that can be tragic. But quite apart from such irony, the mere picture of the grotesque gravedigger, the black-clad prince, and the skull is a picture in the strongest sense picturesque. Caliban and the two shipwrecked drunkards are an admirable symbol; but they are also an admirable scene. Bottom, with the ass's head, sitting in a ring of elves, is excellent moving comedy, but also excellent still life. Falstaff with his huge body, Bardolph with his burning nose, are masterpieces of the pen; but they would be fine sketches even for the pencil. King Lear, in the storm, is a landscape as well as a character study. There is something decorative even about the insistence on the swarthiness of Othello, or the deformity of Richard III.   Shakespeare's work is much more than picturesque; but it is picturesque.   And the same which is said here of him by way of example is largely true of the highest class of literature.   Dante's *Divine Comedy* is supremely important as a philosophy; but it is important merely as a panorama.   Spenser's *Faery Queen* pleases us as an allegory; but it would please us even as a wall-paper. Stronger still is the case of Chaucer who loved the pure picturesque, which always includes something of what we commonly call the ugly.   The huge stature and startling scarlet face of the Sompnour is in just the same spirit as Shakespeare's skulls and motley; the same spirit gave Chaucer's miller bagpipes, and clad his doctor in crimson.   It is the spirit which, while making many other things, loves to make a picture.

Now the second thing to be remarked in apology for the picturesque is, that the very thing which makes it seem trivial ought really to make it seem important; I mean the fact that it consists necessarily of contrasts. It brings together types that stand out from their background, but are abruptly different from each other, like the clown among the fairies or the fool in the forest.   And his audacious reconciliation is a mark not of frivolity but of extreme seriousness.   A man who deals in harmonies, who only matches stars with angels or lambs with spring flowers, he indeed may be frivolous; for he is taking one mood at a time, and perhaps forgetting each mood as it passes.   But a man who ventures to combine an angel and an octopus must have some serious view of the universe.   The man who

should write a dialogue between two early Christians
might be a mere writer of dialogues. But a man who
should write a dialogue between an early Christian and
the Missing Link would have to be a philosopher. The
more widely different the types talked of, the more
serious and universal must be the philosophy which
talks of them. The mark of the light and thoughtless
writer is the harmony of his subject matter; the mark
of the thoughtful writer is its apparent diversity. The
most flippant lyric poet might write a pretty poem
about lambs; but it requires something bolder and
graver than a poet, it requires an ecstatic prophet, to
talk about the lion lying down with the lamb.

Dickens, at any rate, strongly supports this conception: that great literary men as such do not despise the
purely pictorial. No man's works have so much the
quality of illustrating themselves. Few men's works
have been more thoroughly and eagerly illustrated; few
men's works can it have been better fun to illustrate.
As a rule this fascinating quality in the more fantastic
figures of the tale was inseparable from their farcical
quality in the tale. Stiggins's red nose is distinctly
connected with the fact that he is a member of the
Ebenezer Temperance Association; Quilp is little,
because a little of him goes a long way. Mr. Carker
smiles and smiles and is a villain; Mr. Chadband is
fat because in his case to be fat is to be hated. The
story is immeasurably more important than the picture; it is not mere indulgence in the picturesque.
Generally it is an intellectual love of the comic; not a
pure love of the grotesque.

But in one book Dickens suddenly confesses that he

likes the grotesque even without the comic. In one case he makes clear that he enjoys pure pictures with a pure love of the picturesque. That place is *Barnaby Rudge*. There had indeed been hints of it in many episodes in his books; notably, for example, in that fine scene of the death of Quilp—a scene in which the dwarf remains fantastic long after he has ceased to be in any way funny. Still, the dwarf was meant to be funny. Humour of a horrible kind, but still humour, is the purpose of Quilp's existence and position in the book. Laughter is the object of all his oddities. But laughter is not the object of Barnaby Rudge's oddities. His idiot costume and his ugly raven are used for the purpose of the pure grotesque; solely to make a certain kind of Gothic sketch.

It is commonly this love of pictures that drives men back upon the historical novel. But it is very typical of Dickens's living interest in his own time, that though he wrote two historical novels they were neither of them of very ancient history. They were both, indeed, of very recent history; only they were those parts of recent history which were specially picturesque. I do not think that this was due to any mere consciousness on his part that he knew no history. Undoubtedly he knew no history; and he may or may not have been conscious of the fact. But the consciousness did not prevent him from writing a *History of England*. Nor did it prevent him from interlarding all or any of his works with tales of the pictorial past, such as the tale of the broken swords in *Master Humphrey's Clock*, or the indefensibly delightful nightmare of the lady in the stage-coach, which helps to soften the amiable end

of Pickwick. Neither, worst of all, did it prevent him
from dogmatising anywhere and everywhere about
the past, of which he knew nothing; it did not prevent
him from telling the bells to tell Trotty Veck that the
Middle Ages were a failure, nor from solemnly declaring
that the best thing that the mediæval monks ever did
was to create the mean and snobbish quietude of a
modern cathedral city. No, it was not historical
reverence that held him back from dealing with the
remote past; but rather something much better—a
living interest in the living century in which he was
born. He would have thought himself quite intel-
lectually capable of writing a novel about the Council
of Trent or the First Crusade. He would have thought
himself quite equal to analysing the psychology of
Abelard or giving a bright, satiric sketch of St. Augustine. It must frankly be confessed that it was not a
sense of his own unworthiness that held him back; I
fear it was rather a sense of St. Augustine's unworthiness. He could not see the point of any history before
the first slow swell of the French Revolution. He could
understand the revolutions of the eighteenth century;
all the other revolutions of history (so many and so
splendid) were unmeaning to him. But the revolutions
of the eighteenth century he did understand; and to
them therefore he went back, as all historical novelists
go back, in search of the picturesque. And from this
fact an important result follows.

The result that follows is this: that his only two
historical novels are both tales of revolutions—of
eighteenth-century revolutions. These two eighteenth-
century revolutions may seem to differ, and perhaps

do differ in everything except in being revolutions and
of the eighteenth century. The French Revolution,
which is the theme of *A Tale of Two Cities*, was a
revolt in favour of all that is now called enlightenment
and liberation. The great Gordon Riot, which is the
theme of *Barnaby Rudge*, was a revolt in favour of
something which would now be called mere ignorant
and obscurantist Protestantism. Nevertheless both
belonged more typically to the age out of which Dickens
came—the great sceptical and yet creative eighteenth
century of Europe. Whether the mob rose on the
right side or the wrong they both belonged to the time
in which a mob could rise, in which a mob could con-
quer. No growth of intellectual science or of moral
cowardice had made it impossible to fight in the streets,
whether for the republic or for the Bible. If we wish
to know what was the real link, existing actually in
ultimate truth, existing unconsciously in Dickens's
mind, which connected the Gordon Riots with the
French Revolution, the link may be defined though not
with any great adequacy. The nearest and truest
way of stating it is that neither of the two could
possibly happen in Fleet Street to-morrow evening.

Another point of resemblance between the two
books might be found in the fact that they both contain
the sketch of the same kind of eighteenth-century
aristocrat, if indeed that kind of aristocrat really
existed in the eighteenth century. The diabolical dandy
with the rapier and the sneer is at any rate a necessity
of all normal plays and romances; hence Mr. Chester
has a right to exist in this romance, and Foulon a right
to exist in a page of history almost as cloudy and dis-

putable as a romance. What Dickens and other romancers do probably omit from the picture of the eighteenth-century oligarch is probably his liberality. It must never be forgotten that even when he was a despot in practice he was generally a liberal in theory. Dickens and romancers make the pre-revolution tyrant a sincere believer in tyranny; generally he was not. He was a sceptic about everything, even about his own position. The romantic Foulon says of the people, "Let them eat grass," with bitter and deliberate contempt. The real Foulon (if he ever said it at all) probably said it as a sort of dreary joke because he could n't think of any other way out of the problem. Similiarly Mr. Chester, a cynic as he is, believes seriously in the beauty of being a gentleman; a real man of that type probably disbelieved in that as in everything else. Dickens was too bracing, one may say too bouncing himself to understand the psychology of fatigue in a protected and leisured class. He could understand a tyrant like Quilp, a tyrant who is on his throne because he has climbed up into it, like a monkey. He could not understand a tyrant who is on his throne because he is too weary to get out of it. The old aristocrats were in a dead way quite good-natured. They were even humanitarians; which perhaps accounts for the extent to which they roused against themselves the healthy hatred of humanity. But they were tired humanitarians; tired with doing nothing. Figures like that of Mr. Chester, therefore, fail somewhat to give the true sense of something hopeless and helpless which led men to despair of the upper class. He has a boyish pleasure in play-acting; he has an interest in life; being

a villain is his hobby. But the true man of that type
had found all hobbies fail him. He had wearied of
himself as he had wearied of a hundred women. He
was graceful and could not even admire himself in the
glass. He was witty and could not even laugh at his
own jokes. Dickens could never understand tedium.

There is no mark more strange and perhaps sinister
of the interesting and not very sane condition of our
modern literature, than the fact that tedium has been
admirably described in it. Our best modern writers
are never so exciting as they are about dulness. Mr.
Rudyard Kipling is never so powerful as when he is
painting yawning deserts, aching silences, sleepless
nights, or infernal isolation. The excitement in one
of the stories of Mr. Henry James becomes tense,
thrilling, and almost intolerable in all the half hours
during which nothing whatever is said or done. We
are entering again into the mind, into the real mind
of Foulon and Mr. Chester. We begin to understand
the deep despair of those tyrants whom our fathers
pulled down. But Dickens could never have understood that despair; it was not in his soul. And it is
an interesting coincidence that here, in this book of
Barnaby Rudge, there is a character meant to be wholly
grotesque, who, nevertheless, expresses much of that
element in Dickens which prevented him from being a
true interpreter of the tired and sceptical aristocrat.

Sim Tappertit is a fool, but a perfectly honourable
fool. It requires some sincerity to pose. Posing
means that one has not dried up in oneself all the
youthful and innocent vanities with the slow paralysis
of mere pride. Posing means that one is still fresh

enough to enjoy the good opinion of one's fellows.
On the other hand, the true cynic has not enough truth
in him to attempt affectation; he has never even seen
the truth, far less tried to imitate it. Now we might
very well take the type of Mr. Chester on the one hand,
and of Sim Tappertit on the other, as marking the
issue, the conflict, and the victory which really ushered
in the nineteenth century. Dickens was very like Sim
Tappertit. The Liberal Revolution was very like a
Sim Tappertit revolution. It was vulgar, it was over-
done, it was absurd, but it was alive. Dickens was
vulgar, was absurd, overdid everything, but he was alive.
The aristocrats were perfectly correct, but quite dead;
dead long before they were guillotined. The classics
and critics who lamented that Dickens was no gentleman were quite right, but quite dead. The revolution
thought itself rational; but so did Sim Tappertit. It
was really a huge revolt of romanticism against a
reason which had grown sick even of itself. Sim
Tappertit rose against Mr. Chester; and, thank God!
he put his foot upon his neck.

AMERICAN NOTES

American Notes was written soon after Dickens had returned from his first visit to America. That visit had, of course, been a great epoch in his life; but how much of an epoch men did not truly realise until, some time after, in the middle of a quiet story about Salisbury and a ridiculous architect, his feelings flamed out and flared up to the stars in *Martin Chuzzlewit*. The *American Notes* are, however, interesting, because in them he betrays his feelings when he does not know that he is betraying them. Dickens's first visit to America was, from his own point of view, and at the beginning, a happy and festive experiment. It is very characteristic of him that he went among the Americans, enjoyed them, even admired them, and then had a quarrel with them. Nothing was ever so unmistakable as his good-will, except his ill-will; and they were never far apart. And this was not, as some bloodless moderns have sneeringly insinuated, a mere repetition of the proximity between the benevolent stage and the quarrelsome stage of drink. It was a piece of pure optimism; he believed so readily that men were going to be good to him that an injury to him was something more than an injury: it was a shock. What was the exact nature of the American shock must, however, be more carefully stated.

The famous quarrel between Dickens and America, which finds its most elaborate expression in *American Notes*, though its most brilliant expression in *Martin Chuzzlewit*, is an incident about which a great deal remains to be said. But the thing which most specially remains to be said is this. This old Anglo-American quarrel was much more fundamentally friendly than most Anglo-American alliances. In Dickens's day each nation understood the other enough to argue. In our time neither nation understands itself even enough to quarrel. There was an English tradition, from Fox and eighteenth-century England; there was an American tradition from Franklin and eighteenth-century America; and they were still close enough together to discuss their differences with acrimony, perhaps, but with certain fundamental understandings. The eighteenth-century belief in a liberal civilisation was still a dogma; for dogma is the only thing that makes argument or reasoning possible. America, under all its swagger, did still really believe that Europe was its fountain and its mother, because Europe was more fully civilised. Dickens, under all his disgust, did still believe that America was in advance of Europe, because it was more democratic. It was an age, in short, in which the word "progress" could still be used reasonably; because the whole world looked to one way of escape and there was only one kind of progress under discussion. Now, of course, "progress" is a useless word; for progress takes for granted an already defined direction; and it is exactly about the direction that we disagree. Do not let us therefore be misled into any mistaken optimism or special self-congratulation

upon what many people would call the improved relations between England and America.   The relations are
improved because America has finally become a foreign
country.   And with foreign countries all sane men take
care to exchange a certain consideration and courtesy.
But even as late as the time of Dickens's first visit to
the United States, we English still felt America as a
colony; an insolent, offensive, and even unintelligible
colony sometimes, but still a colony; a part of our
civilisation, a limb of our life.   And America itself,
as I have said, under all its bounce and independence,
really regarded us as a mother country.   This being
the case it was possible for us to quarrel, like kinsmen.
Now we only bow and smile, like strangers.

   This tone, as a sort of family responsibility, can be
felt quite specially all through the satires or suggestions
of these *American Notes*.   Dickens is cross with
America because he is worried about America; as if
he were its father.   He explores its industrial, legal,
and educational arrangements like a mother looking
at the housekeeping of a married son; he makes suggestions with a certain acidity; he takes a strange
pleasure in being pessimistic.   He advises them to
take note of how much better certain things are done
in England.   All this is very different from Dickens's
characteristic way of dealing with a foreign country.
In countries really foreign, such as France, Switzer-
land, and Italy, he had two attitudes, neither of them
in the least worried or paternal.   When he found a
thing in Europe which he did not understand, such as
the Roman Catholic Church, he simply called it an old-
world superstition, and sat looking at it like a moonlit

ruin. When he found something that he did understand, such as luncheon baskets, he burst into carols of praise over the superior sense in our civilisation and good management to Continental methods. An example of the first attitude may be found in one of his letters, in which he describes the backwardness and idleness of Catholics who would not build a Birmingham in Italy. He seems quite unconscious of the obvious truth, that the backwardness of Catholics was simply the refusal of Bob Cratchit to enter the house of Gradgrind. An example of the second attitude can be found in the purple patches of fun in *Mugby Junction;* in which the English waitress denounces the profligate French habit of providing new bread and clean food for people travelling by rail. The point is, however, that in neither case has he the air of one suggesting improvements or sharing a problem with the people engaged on it. He does not go carefully with a notebook through Jesuit schools nor offer friendly suggestions to the governors of Parisian prisons. Or if he does, it is in a different spirit; it is in the spirit of an ordinary tourist being shown over the Coliseum or the Pyramids. But he visited America in the spirit of a Government inspector dealing with something it was his duty to inspect. This is never felt either in his praise or blame of Continental countries. When he did not leave a foreign country to decay like a dead dog, he merely watched it at play like a kitten. France he mistook for a kitten. Italy he mistook for a dead dog.

But with America he could feel—and fear. There he could hate, because he could love. There he could feel not the past alone nor the present, but the future also; and, like all brave men, when he saw the future he was a little afraid of it. For of all tests by which the good citizen and strong reformer can be distinguished from the vague faddist or the inhuman sceptic, I know no better test than this—that the unreal reformer sees in front of him one certain future, the future of his fad; while the real reformer sees before him ten or twenty futures among which his country must choose, and may, in some dreadful hour, choose the wrong one. The true patriot is always doubtful of victory; because he knows that he is dealing with a living thing; a thing with free will. To be certain of free will is to be uncertain of success.

The subject matter of the real difference of opinion between Dickens and the public of America can only be understood if it is thus treated as a dispute between brothers about the destiny of a common heritage. The point at issue might be stated like this. Dickens, on his side, did not in his heart doubt for a moment that England would eventually follow America along the road towards real political equality and purely republican institutions. He lived, it must be remembered, before the revival of aristocracy, which has since overwhelmed us—the revival of aristocracy worked through popular science and commercial dictatorship, and which has nowhere been more manifest than in America itself. He knew nothing of this; in his heart he conceded to the Yankees that not only was their revolution right but would ultimately be completed everywhere. But on the other hand, his whole point against the American experiment was this—that if it ignored certain ancient

English contributions it would go to pieces for lack of them. Of these the first was good manners and the second individual liberty—liberty, that is, to speak and write against the trend of the majority. In these things he was much more serious and much more sensible than it is the fashion to think he was; he was indeed one of the most serious and sensible critics England ever had of current and present problems, though his criticism is useless to the point of nonentity about all things remote from him in style of civilisation or in time. His point about good manners is really important. All his grumblings through this book of *American Notes*, all his shrieking satire in *Martin Chuzzlewit* are expressions of a grave and reasonable fear he had touching the future of democracy. And remember again what has been already remarked—instinctively he paid America the compliment of looking at her as the future of democracy.

The mistake which he attacked still exists. I cannot imagine why it is that social equality is somehow supposed to mean social familiarity. Why should equality mean that all men are equally rude? Should it not rather mean that all men are equally polite? Might it not quite reasonably mean that all men should be equally ceremonious and stately and pontifical? What is there specially Equalitarian, for instance, in calling your political friends and even your political enemies by their Christian names in public? There is something very futile in the way in which certain Socialist leaders call each other Tom, Dick, and Harry; especially when Tom is accusing Harry of having basely imposed upon the well-known imbecility of Dick. There is

something quite undemocratic in all men calling each
other by the special and affectionate term "comrade";
especially when they say it with a sneer and smart
inquiry about the funds. Democracy would be quite
satisfied if every man called every other man "sir."
Democracy would have no conceivable reason to complain if every man called every other man "your
excellency" or "your holiness" or "brother of the sun
and moon." The only democratic essential is that it
should be a term of dignity and that it should be given
to all. To abolish all terms of dignity is no more
specially democratic than the Roman emperor's wish
to cut off everybody's head at once was specially democratic. That involved equality certainly, but it was
lacking in respect.

Dickens saw America as markedly the seat of this
danger. He saw that there was a perilous possibility
that republican ideals might be allied to a social anarchy
good neither for them nor for any other ideals. Republican simplicity, which is difficult, might be quickly
turned into Bohemian brutality, which is easy. Cin-
cinnatus, instead of putting his hand to the plough,
might put his feet on the tablecloth, and an impression
prevail that it was all a part of the same rugged equality
and freedom. Insolence might become a tradition.
Bad manners might have all the sanctity of good
manners. "There you are!" cries Martin Chuzzlewit
indignantly, when the American has befouled the
butter. "A man deliberately makes a hog of himself
and *that* is an Institution." But the thread of thought
which we must always keep in hand in this matter is
that he would not thus have worried about the degrada-

tion of republican simplicity into general rudeness if he had not from first to last instinctively felt that America held human democracy in her hand, to exalt it or to let it fall. In one of his gloomier moments he wrote down his fear that the greatest blow ever struck at liberty would be struck by America in the failure of her mission upon the earth.

This brings us to the other ground of his alarm—the matter of liberty of speech. Here also he was much more reasonable and philosophic than has commonly been realised. The truth is that the lurid individualism of Carlyle has, with its violent colours, "killed" the tones of most criticism of his time; and just as we can often see a scheme of decoration better if we cover some flaming picture, so you can judge nineteenth-century England much better if you leave Carlyle out. He is important to moderns because he led that return to Toryism which has been the chief feature of modernity, but his judgments were often not only spiritually false, but really quite superficial. Dickens understood the danger of democracy far better than Carlyle; just as he understood the merits of democracy far better than Carlyle. And of this fact we can produce one plain evidence in the matter of which we speak. Carlyle, in his general dislike of the revolutionary movement, lumped liberty and democracy together and said that the chief objection to democracy was that it involved the excess and misuse of liberty; he called democracy "anarchy or no-rule." Dickens, with far more philosophical insight and spiritual delicacy, saw that the real danger of democracy is that it tends to the very opposite of anarchy; even to the very opposite of liberty.

He lamented in America the freedom of manners.
But he lamented even more the absence of freedom of
opinion. "I believe there is no country on the face
of the earth," he says, "where there is less freedom of
opinion on any subject in reference to which there is
a broad difference of opinion than in this. There!
I write the words with reluctance, disappointment,
and sorrow; but I believe it from the bottom of my
soul. The notion that I, a man alone by myself in
America, should venture to suggest to the Americans
that there was one point on which they were neither
just to their own countrymen nor to us, actually
struck the boldest dumb! Washington Irving, Prescott,
Hoffman, Bryant, Halleck, Dana, Washington Allston
—every man who writes in this country is devoted to
the question, and not one of them *dares* to raise his
voice and complain of the atrocious state of the law.
The wonder is that a breathing man can be found
with temerity enough to suggest to the Americans the
possibility of their having done wrong. I wish you
could have seen the faces that I saw down both sides of
the table at Hartford when I began to talk about Scott.
I wish you could have heard how I gave it out. My
blood so boiled when I thought of the monstrous injustice that I felt as if I were twelve feet high when
I thrust it down their throats." Dickens knew no
history, but he had all history behind him in feeling
that a pure democracy does tend, when it goes wrong,
to be too traditional and absolute. The truth is indeed
a singular example of the unfair attack upon democracy
in our own time. Everybody can repeat the platitude
that the mob can be the greatest of all tyrants. But

few realise or remember the corresponding truth which goes along with it—that the mob is the only permanent and unassailable high priest. Democracy drives its traditions too hard; but democracy is the only thing that keeps any traditions. An aristocracy must always be going after some new thing. The severity of democracy is far more of a virtue than its liberty. The decorum of a democracy is far more of a danger than its lawlessness. Dickens discovered this in his great quarrels about the copyright, when a whole nation acted on a small point of opinion as if it were going to lynch him. But, fortunately for the purpose of this argument, there is no need to go back to the forties for such a case. Another great literary man has of late visited America; and it is possible that Maxim Gorky may be in a position to state how far democracy is likely to err on the side of mere liberty and laxity. He may have found, like Dickens, some freedom of manners; he did not find much freedom of morals.

Along with such American criticism should really go his very characteristic summary of the question of the Red Indian. It marks the combination between the mental narrowness and the moral justice of the old Liberal. Dickens can see nothing in the Red Indian except that he is barbaric, retrograde, bellicose, uncleanly, and superstitious—in short, that he is not a member of the special civilisation of Birmingham or Brighton. It is curious to note the contrast between the cheery, nay Cockney, contempt with which Dickens speaks of the American Indian and that chivalrous and pathetic essay in which Washington Irving celebrates the virtues of the vanishing race. Between Washington

Irving and his friend Charles Dickens there was always indeed this ironical comedy of inversion. It is amusing that the Englishman should have been the pushing and even pert modernist, and the American the stately antiquarian and lover of lost causes. But while a man of more mellow sympathies may well dislike Dickens's dislike of savages, and even disdain his disdain, he ought to sharply remind himself of the admirable ethical fairness and equity which meet with that restricted outlook. In the very act of describing Red Indians as devils who, like so much dirt, it would pay us to sweep away, he pauses to deny emphatically that we have any right to sweep them away. We have no right to wrong the man, he means to say, even if he himself be a kind of wrong. Here we strike the ringing iron of the old conscience and sense of honour which marked the best men of his party and of his epoch. This rigid and even reluctant justice towers, at any rate, far above modern views of savages, above the sentimentalism of the mere humanitarian and the far weaker sentimentalism that pleads for brutality and a race war. Dickens was at least more of a man than the brutalitarian who claims to wrong people because they are nasty, or the humanitarian who cannot be just to them without pretending that they are nice.

PICTURES FROM ITALY

THE *Pictures from Italy* are excellent in themselves and excellent as a foil to the *American Notes*. Here we have none of that air of giving a decision like a judge or sending in a report like an inspector; here we have only glimpses, light and even fantastic glimpses, of a world that is really alien to Dickens. It is so alien that he can almost entirely enjoy it. For no man can entirely enjoy that which he loves; contentment is always unpatriotic. The difference can indeed be put with approximate perfection in one phrase. In Italy he was on a holiday; in America he was on a tour. But indeed Dickens himself has quite sufficiently conveyed the difference in the two phrases that he did actually use for the titles of the two books. Dickens often told unconscious truths, especially in small matters. The *American Notes* really are notes, like the notes of a student or a professional witness. The *Pictures from Italy* are only pictures from Italy, like the miscellaneous pictures that all tourists bring from Italy.

To take another and perhaps closer figure of speech, almost all Dickens's works such as these may best be regarded as private letters addressed to the public. His private correspondence was quite as brilliant as his public works; and many of his public works are almost as formless and casual as his private correspondence.

If he had been struck insensible for a year, I really think that his friends and family could have brought out one of his best books by themselves if they had happened to keep his letters. The homogeneity of his public and private work was indeed strange in many ways. On the one hand, there was little that was pompously and unmistakably public in the publications; on the other hand, there was very little that was private in the private letters. His hilarity had almost a kind of hardness about it; no man's letters, I should think, ever needed less expurgation on the ground of weakness or undue confession. The main part, and certainly the best part, of such a book as *Pictures from Italy* can certainly be criticised best as part of that perpetual torrent of entertaining autobiography which he flung at his children as if they were his readers and his readers as if they were his children. There are some brilliant patches of sense and nonsense in this book; but there is always something accidental in them; as if they might have occurred somewhere else. Perhaps the most attractive of them is the incomparable description of the Italian Marionette Theatre in which they acted a play about the death of Napoleon in St. Helena. The description is better than that of Codlin and Short's Punch and Judy, and almost as good as that of Mrs. Jarley's Wax Works. Indeed the humour is similar; for Punch is supposed to be funny, but Napoleon (as Mrs. Jarley said when asked if her show was funnier than Punch) was not funny at all. The idea of a really tragic scene being enacted between tiny wooden dolls with large heads is delightfully dealt with by Dickens. We can almost imagine

the scene in which the wooden Napoleon haughtily
rebukes his wooden jailor for calling him General Bona-
parte—"Sir Hudson Low, call me not thus; I am
Napoleon, Emperor of the French." There is also
something singularly gratifying about the scene of
Napoleon's death, in which he lay in bed with his little
wooden hands outside the counterpane and the doctor
(who was hung on wires too short) "delivered medical
opinions in the air." It may seem flippant to dwell
on such flippancies in connection with a book which
contains many romantic descriptions and many moral
generalisations which Dickens probably valued highly.
But it is not for such things that he is valued. In all
his writings, from his most reasoned and sustained
novel to his maddest private note, it is always this
obstreperous instinct for farce which stands out as his
in the highest sense. His wisdom is at the best talent,
his foolishness is genius. Just that exuberant levity
which we associate with a moment we associate in his
case with immortality. It is said of certain old ma-
sonry that the mortar was so hard that it has survived
the stones. So if Dickens could revisit the thing he
built, he would be surprised to see all the work he
thought solid and responsible wasted almost utterly
away, but the shortest frivolities and the most momentary jokes remaining like colossal rocks for ever.

MARTIN CHUZZLEWIT

THERE is a certain quality or element which broods over the whole of *Martin Chuzzlewit* to which it is difficult for either friends or foes to put a name. I think the reader who enjoys Dickens's other books has an impression that it is a kind of melancholy. There are grotesque figures of the most gorgeous kind; there are scenes that are farcical even by the standard of the farcical license of Dickens; there is humour both of the heaviest and of the lightest kind; there are two great comic personalities who run like a rich vein through the whole story, Pecksniff and Mrs. Gamp; there is one blinding patch of brilliancy, the satire on American cant; there is Todgers's boarding-house; there is Bailey; there is Mr. Mould, the incomparable undertaker. But yet in spite of everything, in spite even of the undertaker, the book is sad. No one I think ever went to it in that mixed mood of a tired tenderness and a readiness to believe and laugh in which most of Dickens's novels are most enjoyed. We go for a particular novel to Dickens as we go for a particular inn. We go to the sign of the Pickwick Papers. We go to the sign of the Rudge and Raven. We go to the sign of the Old Curiosities. We go to the sign of the Two Cities. We go to each or all of them according to what kind of hospitality and what kind of happiness

we require. But it is always some kind of hospitality
and some kind of happiness that we require. And as
in the case of inns we also remember that while there
was shelter in all and food in all and some kind of fire
and some kind of wine in all, yet one has left upon us an
indescribable and unaccountable memory of mortality
and decay, of dreariness in the rooms and even of taste-
lessness in the banquet. So any one who has enjoyed
the stories of Dickens as they should be enjoyed has a
nameless feeling that this one story is sad and almost
sodden. Dickens himself had this feeling, though his
breezy vanity forbade him to express it in so many
words. In spite of Pecksniff, in spite of Mrs. Gamp,
in spite of the yet greater Bailey, the story went
lumberingly and even lifelessly; he found the sales falling off; he fancied his popularity waning, and by a
sudden impulse most inartistic and yet most artistic,
he dragged in the episode of Martin's visit to America,
which is the blazing jewel and the sudden redemption
of the book. He wrote it at an uneasy and unhappy
period of his life; when he had ceased wandering in
America, but could not cease wandering altogether;
when he had lost his original routine of work which was
violent but regular, and had not yet settled down to the
full enjoyment of his success and his later years. He
poured into this book genius that might make the
mountains laugh, invention that juggled with the stars.
But the book was sad; and he knew it.

The just reason for this is really interesting. Yet
it is one that is not easy to state without guarding
one's self on the one side or the other against great mis-
understandings; and these stipulations or preliminary

allowances must in such a case as this of necessity be
made first.   Dickens was among other things a satirist,
a pure satirist.   I have never been able to understand
why this title is always specially and sacredly reserved
for Thackeray.   Thackeray was a novelist; in the
strict and narrow sense at any rate, Thackeray was a
far greater novelist than Dickens.   But Dickens certainly was the satirist.   The essence of satire is that it
perceives some absurdity inherent in the logic of some
position, and that it draws that absurdity out and
isolates it, so that all can see it.   Thus for instance
when Dickens says, "Lord Coodle would go out; Sir
Thomas Doodle would n't come in; and there being no
people to speak of in England except Coodle and Doodle
the country has been without a Government"; when
Dickens says this he suddenly pounces on and plucks
out the one inherent absurdity in the English party
system which is hidden behind all its paraphernalia of
Parliaments and Statutes, elections and ballot papers.
When all the dignity and all the patriotism and all the
public interest of the English constitutional party
conflict have been fully allowed for, there does remain
the bold, bleak question which Dickens in substance
asks, "Suppose I want somebody else who is neither
Coodle nor Doodle."   This is the great quality called
satire; it is a kind of taunting reasonableness; and it is
inseparable from a certain insane logic which is often
called exaggeration.   Dickens was more of a satirist
than Thackeray for this simple reason: that Thackeray
carried a man's principles as far as that man carried
them; Dickens carried a man's principles as far as
a man's principles would go.   Dickens in short (as

people put it) exaggerated the man and his principles; that is to say he emphasised them. Dickens drew a man's absurdity out of him; Thackeray left a man's absurdity in him. Of this last fact we can take any example we like; take for instance the comparison between the city man as treated by Thackeray in the most satiric of his novels, with the city man as treated by Dickens in one of the mildest and maturest of his. Compare the character of old Mr. Osborne in *Vanity Fair* with the character of Mr. Podsnap in *Our Mutual Friend*. In the case of Mr. Osborne there is nothing except the solid blocking in of a brutal dull convincing character. *Vanity Fair* is not a satire on the City except in so far as it happens to be true. *Vanity Fair* is not a satire on the City, in short, except in so far as the City is a satire on the City. But Mr. Podsnap is a pure satire; he is an extracting out of the City man of those purely intellectual qualities which happen to make that kind of City man a particularly exasperating fool. One might almost say that Mr. Podsnap is all Mr. Osborne's opinions separated from Mr. Osborne and turned into a character. In short the satirist is more purely philosophical than the novelist. The novelist may be only an observer; the satirist must be a thinker. He must be a thinker, he must be a philosophical thinker for this simple reason; that he exercises his philosophical thought in deciding what part of his subject he is to satirise. You may have the dullest possible intelligence and be a portrait painter; but a man must have a serious intellect in order to be a caricaturist. He has to select what thing he will caricature. True satire is always of this intellectual

kind; true satire is always, so to speak, a variation
or fantasia upon the air of pure logic. The satirist
is the man who carries men's enthusiasm further than
they carry it themselves. He outstrips the most
extravagant fanatic. He is years ahead of the most
audacious prophet. He sees where men's detached
intellect will eventually lead them, and he tells them
the name of the place—which is generally hell.

Now of this detached and rational use of satire there
is one great example in this book. Even *Gulliver's
Travels* is hardly more reasonable than Martin Chuzzlewit's travels in the incredible land of the Americans.
Before considering the humour of this description in its
more exhaustive and liberal aspects, it may be first remarked that in this American part of *Martin Chuzzlewit*, Dickens quite specially sharpens up his own mere
controversial and political intelligence. There are
more things here than anywhere else in Dickens that
partake of the nature of pamphleteering, of positive
challenge, of sudden repartee, of pugnacious and exasperating query, in a word of everything that belongs
to the pure art of controversy as distinct not only from
the pure art of fiction but even also from the pure art
of satire. I am inclined to think (to put the matter
not only shortly but clumsily) that Dickens was never
in all his life so strictly clever as he is in the American
part of *Martin Chuzzlewit*. There are places where he
was more inspired, almost in the sense of being intoxi-
cated, as, for instance, in the Micawber feasts of *David
Copperfield;* there are places where he wrote more
carefully and cunningly, as, for instance, in the mystery
of *The Mystery of Edwin Drood;* there are places where

he wrote very much more humanly, more close to the
ground and to growing things, as in the whole of that
admirable book *Great Expectations*. But I do not
think that his mere abstract acuteness and rapidity of
thought were ever exercised with such startling exactitude as they are in this place in *Martin Chuzzlewit*.
It is to be noted, for instance, that his American
experience had actually worked him up to a heat and
habit of argument. A slave-owner in the Southern
States tells Dickens that slave-owners do not ill-treat
their slaves, that it is not to the interest of slave-owners
to ill-treat their slaves. Dickens flashes back that it is
not to the interest of a man to get drunk, but he does
get drunk. This pugnacious atmosphere of parry and
riposte must first of all be allowed for and understood in
all the satiric excursus of Martin in America. Dickens
is arguing all the time; and, to do him justice, arguing
very well. These chapters are full not merely of
exuberant satire on America in the sense that Dotheboys Hall or Mr. Bumble's Workhouse are exuberant
satires on England. They are full also of sharp argument with America as if the man who wrote expected
retort and was prepared with rejoinder. The rest of
the book, like the rest of Dickens's books, possesses
humour. This part of the book, like hardly any of
Dickens's books, possesses wit. The republican gentleman who receives Martin on landing is horrified on
hearing an English servant speak of the employer as
"the master." "There are no masters in America,"
says the gentleman. "All owners are they?" says
Martin. This sort of verbal promptitude is out of
the ordinary scope of Dickens; but we find it frequently

in this particular part of *Martin Chuzzlewit*. Martin himself is constantly breaking out into a controversial lucidity, which is elsewhere not at all a part of his character. When they talk to him about the institutions of America he asks sarcastically whether bowie knives and swordsticks and revolvers are the institutions of America. All this (if I may summarise) is expressive of one main fact. Being a satirist means being a philosopher. Dickens was not always very philosophical; but he had this permanent quality of the philosopher about him, that he always remembered people by their opinions. Elijah Pogram was to him the man who said that "his boastful answer to the tyrant and the despot was that his bright home was the land of the settin' sun." Mr. Scadder and Mr. Jefferson Brick were to him the men who said (in co-operation) that "the libation of freedom must sometimes be quaffed in blood." And in these chapters more than anywhere else he falls into the extreme habit of satire, that of treating people as if there were nothing about them except their opinions. It is therefore difficult to accept these pages as pages in a novel, splendid as they are considered as pages in a parody. I do not dispute that men have said and do say that "the libation of freedom must sometimes be quaffed in blood," that "their bright homes are the land of the settin' sun," that "they taunt that lion," that "alone they dare him," or "that softly sleeps the calm ideal in the whispering chambers of imagination." I have read too much American journalism to deny that any of these sentences and any of these opinions may at some time or other have been uttered. I do not deny

that there are such opinions. But I do deny that
there are such people. Elijah Pogram had some other
business in life besides defending defaulting post-
masters; he must have been a son or a father or a
husband or at least (admirable thought) a lover. Mr.
Chollop had some moments in his existence when he
was not threatening his fellow-creatures with his sword-
stick and his revolver. Of all this human side of
such American types Dickens does not really give any
hint at all. He does not suggest that the bully Chollop
had even such coarse good-humour as bullies almost
always have. He does not suggest that the humbug
Elijah Pogram had even as much greasy amiability
as humbugs almost invariably have. He is not studying them as human beings, even as bad human beings;
he is studying them as conceptions, as points of view, as
symbols of a state of mind with which he is in violent
disagreement. To put it roughly, he is not describing
characters, he is satirising fads. To put it more exactly,
he is not describing characters; he is persecuting
heresies. There is one thing really to be said against
his American satire; it is a serious thing to be said: it is
an argument, and it is true. This can be said of
Martin's wanderings in America, that from the time
he lands in America to the time he sets sail from it he
never meets a living man. He has travelled in the
land of Laputa. All the people he has met have
been absurd opinions walking about. The whole art
of Dickens in such passages as these consisted in one
thing. It consisted in finding an opinion that had not
a leg to stand on, and then giving it two legs to stand
on.

So much may be allowed; it may be admitted that Dickens is in this sense the great satirist, in that he can imagine absurd opinions walking by themselves about the street. It may be admitted that Thackeray would not have allowed an absurd opinion to walk about the street without at least tying a man on to it for the sake of safety. But while this first truth may be evident, the second truth which is the complement of it may easily be forgotten. On the one hand there was no man who could so much enjoy mere intellectual satire apart from humanity as Dickens. On the other hand there was no man who, with another and more turbulent part of his nature, demanded humanity, and demanded its supremacy over intellect, more than Dickens. To put it shortly: there never was a man so much fitted for saying that everything was wrong; and there never was a man who was so desirous of saying that everything was right. Thus, when he met men with whom he violently disagreed, he described them as devils or lunatics; he could not bear to describe them as men. If they could not think with him on essentials he could not stand the idea that they were human souls; he cast them out; he forgot them; and if he could not forget them he caricatured them. He was too emotional to regard them as anything but enemies, if they were not friends. He was too humane not to hate them. Charles Lamb said with his inimitable sleek pungency that he could read all the books there were; he excluded books that obviously were not books, as cookery books, chessboards bound so as to look like books, and all the works of modern historians and philosophers. One might say in much the same style that Dickens loved all the men in the world; that is he loved all the men whom he was able to recognise as men; the rest he turned into griffins and chimeras without any serious semblance to humanity. Even in his books he never hates a human being. If he wishes to hate him he adopts the simple expedient of making him an inhuman being. Now of these two strands almost the whole of Dickens is made up; they are not only different strands, they are even antagonistic strands. I mean that the whole of Dickens is made up of the strand of satire and the strand of sentimentalism; and the strand of satire is quite unnecessarily merciless and hostile, and the strand of sentimentalism is quite unnecessarily humanitarian and even maudlin. On the proper interweaving of these two things depends the great part of Dickens's success in a novel. And by the consideration of them we can probably best arrive at the solution of the particular emotional enigma of the novel called *Martin Chuzzlewit*.

Martin Chuzzlewit is, I think, vaguely unsatisfactory to the reader, vaguely sad and heavy even to the reader who loves Dickens, because in *Martin Chuzzlewit* more than anywhere else in Dickens's works, more even than in *Oliver Twist*, there is a predominance of the harsh and hostile sort of humour over the hilarious and the humane. It is absurd to lay down any such little rules for the testing of literature. But this may be broadly said and yet with confidence: that Dickens is always at his best when he is laughing at the people whom he really admires. He is at his most humorous in writing of Mr. Pickwick, who represents passive virtue. He is at his most humorous in writing of Mr.

Sam Weller, who represents active virtue. He is never so funny as when he is speaking of people in whom fun itself is a virtue, like the poor people in the Fleet or the Marshalsea. And in the stories that had immediately preceded *Martin Chuzzlewit* he had consistently concerned himself in the majority of cases with the study of such genial and honourable eccentrics; if they are lunatics they are amiable lunatics. In the last important novel before *Martin Chuzzlewit*, *Barnaby Rudge*, the hero himself is an amiable lunatic. In the novel before that, *The Old Curiosity Shop*, the two comic figures, Dick Swiveller and the Marchioness, are not only the most really entertaining, but also the most really sympathetic characters in the book. Before that came *Oliver Twist* (which is, I have said, an exception), and before that *Pickwick*, where the hero is, as Mr. Weller says, "an angel in gaiters." Hitherto, then, on the whole, the central Dickens character had been the man who gave to the poor many things, gold and wine and feasting and good advice; but among other things gave them a good laugh at himself. The jolly old English merchant of the Pickwick type was popular on both counts. People liked to see him throw his money in the gutter. They also liked to see him throw himself there occasionally. In both acts they recognised a common quality of virtue.

Now I think it is certainly the disadvantage of *Martin Chuzzlewit* that none of its absurd characters are thus sympathetic. There are in the book two celebrated characters who are both especially exuberant and amusing even for Dickens, and who are both especially heartless and abominable even for Dickens—

I mean of course Mr. Pecksniff on the one hand and
Mrs. Gamp on the other. The humour of both of
them is gigantesque. Nobody will ever forget the first
time he read the words " Now I should be very glad
to see Mrs. Todgers's idea of a wooden leg." It is
like remembering first love: there is still some sort of
ancient sweetness and sting. I am afraid that, in spite
of many criticisms to the contrary, I am still unable
to take Mr. Pecksniff's hypocrisy seriously. He does
not seem to me so much a hypocrite as a rhetorician;
he reminds me of Serjeant Buzfuz. A very capable
critic, Mr. Noyes, said that I was wrong when I suggested in another place that Dickens must have loved
Pecksniff. Mr. Noyes thinks it clear that Dickens
hated Pecksniff. I cannot believe it. Hatred does
indeed linger round its object as much as love; but
not in that way. Dickens is always making Pecksniff
say things which have a wild poetical truth about
them. Hatred allows no such outbursts of original
innocence. But however that may be the broad fact
remains—Dickens may or may not have loved Pecksniff
comically, but he did not love him seriously; he did not
respect him as he certainly respected Sam Weller.
The same of course is true of Mrs. Gamp. To any one
who appreciates her unctuous and sumptuous conversation it is difficult indeed not to feel that it would
be almost better to be killed by Mrs. Gamp than to be
saved by a better nurse. But the fact remains. In
this book Dickens has not allowed us to love the most
absurd people seriously, and absurd people ought to be
loved seriously. Pecksniff has to be amusing all the
time; the instant he ceases to be laughable he becomes

detestable.   Pickwick can take his ease at his inn; he
can be leisurely, he can be spacious; he can fall into
moods of gravity and even of dulness; he is not bound
to be always funny or to forfeit the reader's concern, for
he is a good man, and therefore even his dulness is
beautiful, just as is the dulness of the animal.   We can
leave Pickwick a little while by the fire to think; for the
thoughts of Pickwick, even if they were to go slowly,
would be full of all the things that all men care for—
old friends and old inns and memory and the goodness
of God.   But we dare not leave Pecksniff alone for a
moment.   We dare not leave him thinking by the
fire, for the thoughts of Pecksniff would be too frightful.

CHRISTMAS BOOKS

THE mystery of Christmas is in a manner identical
with the mystery of Dickens. If ever we adequately
explain the one we may adequately explain the other.
And indeed, in the treatment of the two, the chronological or historical order must in some degree be remembered. Before we come to the question of what Dickens
did for Christmas we must consider the question of what
Christmas did for Dickens. How did it happen that
this bustling, nineteenth-century man, full of the almost
cock-sure common-sense of the utilitarian and liberal
epoch, came to associate his name chiefly in literary
history with the perpetuation of a half pagan and half
Catholic festival which he would certainly have called
an antiquity and might easily have called a superstition?
Christmas has indeed been celebrated before in English
literature; but it had, in the most noticeable cases, been
celebrated in connection with that kind of feudalism
with which Dickens would have severed his connection
with an ignorant and even excessive scorn. Sir Roger
de Coverley kept Christmas; but it was a feudal
Christmas. Sir Walter Scott sang in praise of Christmas; but it was a feudal Christmas. And Dickens
was not only indifferent to the dignity of the old
country gentleman or to the genial archæology of Scott;

he was even harshly and insolently hostile to it. If
Dickens had lived in the neighbourhood of Sir Roger de
Coverley he would undoubtedly, like Tom Touchy,
have been always "having the law of him." If
Dickens had stumbled in among the old armour and
quiant folios of Scott's study he would certainly have
read his brother novelist a lesson in no measured terms
about the futility of thus fumbling in the dust-bins of
old oppression and error. So far from Dickens being
one of those who like a thing because it is old, he was
one of those cruder kind of reformers, in theory at
least, who actually dislike a thing because it is old.
He was not merely the more righteous kind of Radical
who tries to uproot abuses; he was partly also that more
suicidal kind of Radical who tries to uproot himself. In
theory at any rate, he had no adequate conception of
the importance of human tradition; in his time it had
been twisted and falsified into the form of an opposition
to democracy. In truth, of course, tradition is the
most democratic of all things, for tradition is merely a
democracy of the dead as well as the living. But
Dickens and his special group or generation had no
grasp of this permanent position; they had been called
to a special war for the righting of special wrongs. In
so far as such an institution as Christmas was old,
Dickens would even have tended to despise it. He
could never have put the matter to himself in the correct
way—that while there are some things whose antiquity
does prove that they are dying, there are some other
things whose antiquity only proves that they cannot
die. If some Radical contemporary and friend of
Dickens had happened to say to him that in defending

the mince-pies and the mummeries of Christmas he
was defending a piece of barbaric and brutal ritualism,
doomed to disappear in the light of reason along with
the Boy-Bishop and the Lord of Misrule, I am not
sure that Dickens (though he was one of the readiest
and most rapid masters of reply in history) would have
found it very easy upon his own principles to answer.
It was by a great ancestral instinct that he defended
Christmas; by that sacred sub-consciousness which is
called tradition, which some have called a dead thing,
but which is really a thing far more living than the
intellect. There is a dark kinship and brotherhood of
all mankind which is much too deep to be called hered-
ity or to be in any way explained in scientific formulæ;
blood is thicker than water and is especially very much
thicker than water on the brain. But this unconscious
and even automatic quality in Dickens's defence of
the Christmas feast, this fact that his defence might
almost be called animal rather than mental, though in
proper language it should be called merely virile; all
this brings us back to the fact that we must begin with
the atmosphere of the subject itself. We must not ask
Dickens what Christmas is, for with all his heat and
eloquence he does not know. Rather we must ask
Christmas what Dickens is—ask how this strange child
of Christmas came to be born out of due time.

Dickens devoted his genius in a somewhat special
sense to the description of happiness. No other literary
man of his eminence has made this central human aim
so specially his subject matter. Happiness is a mystery
—generally a momentary mystery—which seldom stops
long enough to submit itself to artistic observation,

and which, even when it is habitual, has something about it which renders artistic description almost impossible. There are twenty tiny minor poets who can describe fairly impressively an eternity of agony; there are very few even of the eternal poets who can describe ten minutes of satisfaction. Nevertheless, mankind being half divine is always in love with the impossible, and numberless attempts have been made from the beginning of human literature to describe a real state of felicity. Upon the whole, I think, the most successful have been the most frankly physical and symbolic; the flowers of Eden or the jewels of the New Jerusalem. Many writers, for instance, have called the gold and chrysolite of the Holy City a vulgar lump of jewellery. But when these critics themselves attempt to describe their conceptions of future happiness, it is always some priggish nonsense about "planes," about "cycles of fulfilment," or "spirals of spiritual evolution." Now a cycle is just as much a physical metaphor as a flower of Eden; a spiral is just as much a physical metaphor as a precious stone. But, after all, a garden is a beautiful thing; whereas this is by no means necessarily true of a cycle, as can be seen in the case of a bicycle. A jewel, after all, is a beautiful thing; but this is not necessarily so of a spiral, as can be seen in the case of a corkscrew. Nothing is gained by dropping the old material metaphors, which did hint at heavenly beauty, and adopting other material metaphors which do not even give a hint of earthly beauty. This modern or spiral method of describing indescribable happiness may, I think, be dismissed. Then there has been another method

which has been adopted by many men of a very real
poetical genius. It was the method of the old pastoral
poets like Theocritus. It was in another way that
adopted by the elegance and piety of Spenser. It was
certainly expressed in the pictures of Watteau; and it
had a very sympathetic and even manly expression in
modern England in the decorative poetry of William
Morris. These men of genius, from Theocritus to
Morris, occupied themselves in endeavouring to describe
happiness as a state of certain human beings, the atmosphere of a commonwealth, the enduring climate of
certain cities or islands. They poured forth treasures
of the truest kind of imagination upon describing the
happy lives and landscapes of Utopia or Atlantis or
the Earthly Paradise. They traced with the most
tender accuracy the tracery of its fruit-trees or the
glimmering garments of its women; they used every
ingenuity of colour or intricate shape to suggest its
infinite delight. And what they succeeded in suggesting was always its infinite melancholy. William
Morris described the Earthly Paradise in such a way
that the only strong emotional note left on the mind
was the feeling of how homeless his travellers felt in
that alien Elysium; and the reader sympathised with
them, feeling that he would prefer not only Elizabethan
England but even twentieth-century Camberwell to
such a land of shining shadows. Thus literature has
almost always failed in endeavouring to describe happiness as a state. Human tradition, human custom and
folk-lore (though far more true and reliable than literature as a rule) have not often succeeded in giving quite
the correct symbols for a real atmosphere of *camaraderie*

and joy. But here and there the note has been struck with the sudden vibration of the *vox humana*. In human tradition it has been struck chiefly in the old celebrations of Christmas. In literature it has been struck chiefly in Dickens's Christmas tales.

In the historic celebration of Christmas as it remains from Catholic times in certain northern countries (and it is to be remembered that in Catholic times the northern countries were, if possible, more Catholic than anybody else), there are three qualities which explain, I think, its hold upon the human sense of happiness, especially in such men as Dickens. There are three notes of Christmas, so to speak, which are also notes of happiness, and which the pagans and the Utopians forget. If we state what they are in the case of Christmas, it will be quite sufficiently obvious how important they are in the case of Dickens.

The first quality is what may be called the dramatic quality. The happiness is not a state; it is a crisis. All the old customs surrounding the celebration of the birth of Christ are made by human instinct so as to insist and re-insist upon this crucial quality. Everything is so arranged that the whole household may feel, if possible, as a household does when a child is actually being born in it. The thing is a vigil and a vigil with a definite limit. People sit up at night until they hear the bells ring. Or they try to sleep at night in order to see their presents the next morning. Everywhere there is a limitation, a restraint; at one moment the door is shut, at the moment after it is opened. The hour has come or it has not come; the parcels are undone or they are not undone; there is no evolution of

Christmas presents. This sharp and theatrical quality
in pleasure, which human instinct and the mother wit
of the world has wisely put into the popular celebrations
of Christmas, is also a quality which is essential in such
romantic literature as Dickens wrote. In romantic
literature the hero and heroine must indeed be happy,
but they must also be unexpectedly happy. This is
the first connecting link between literature and the old
religious feast; this is the first connecting link between
Dickens and Christmas.

The second element to be found in all such festivity
and all such romance is the element which is represented
as well as it could be represented by the mere fact that
Christmas occurs in the winter. It is the element not
merely of contrast, but actually of antagonism. It
preserves everything that was best in the merely
primitive or pagan view of such ceremonies or such
banquets. If we are carousing, at least we are warriors
carousing. We hang above us, as it were, the shields
and battle-axes with which we must do battle with the
giants of the snow and hail. All comfort must be based
on discomfort. Man chooses when he wishes to be
most joyful the very moment when the whole material
universe is most sad. It is this contradiction and
mystical defiance which gives a quality of manliness
and reality to the old winter feasts which is not characteristic of the sunny felicities of the Earthly Paradise.
And this curious element has been carried out even in all
the trivial jokes and tasks that have always surrounded
such occasions as these. The object of the jovial
customs was not to make everything artificially easy:
on the contrary, it was rather to make everything

artificially difficult. Idealism is not only expressed
by shooting an arrow at the stars; the fundamental
principle of idealism is also expressed by putting a leg
of mutton at the top of a greasy pole. There is in all
such observances a quality which can be called only
the quality of divine obstruction. For instance, in
the game of snapdragon (that admirable occupation)
the conception is that raisins taste much nicer if they
are brands saved from the burning. About all Christmas things there is something a little nobler, if only
nobler in form and theory, than mere comfort; even
holly is prickly. It is not hard to see the connection
of this kind of historic instinct with a romantic writer
like Dickens. The healthy novelist must always play
snapdragon with his principal characters; he must
always be snatching the hero and heroine like raisins
out of the fire.

The third great Christmas element is the element
of the grotesque. The grotesque is the natural expression of joy; and all the Utopias and new Edens
of the poets fail to give a real impression of enjoyment,
very largely because they leave out the grotesque. A
man in most modern Utopias cannot really be happy;
he is too dignified. A man in Morris's Earthly Paradise cannot really be enjoying himself; he is too decorative. When real human beings have real delights they
tend to express them entirely in grotesques—I might
almost say entirely in goblins. On Christmas Eve one
may talk about ghosts so long as they are turnip ghosts.
But one would not be allowed (I hope, in any decent
family) to talk on Christmas Eve about astral bodies.
The boar's head of old Yule-time was as grotesque as

the donkey's head of Bottom the Weaver. But there is only one set of goblins quite wild enough to express the wild goodwill of Christmas. Those goblins are the characters of Dickens.

Arcadian poets and Arcadian painters have striven to express happiness by means of beautiful figures. Dickens understood that happiness is best expressed by ugly figures. In beauty, perhaps, there is something allied to sadness; certainly there is something akin to joy in the grotesque, nay, in the uncouth. There is something mysteriously associated with happiness not only in the corpulence of Falstaff and the corpulence of Tony Weller, but even in the red nose of Bardolph or the red nose of Mr. Stiggins. A thing of beauty is an inspiration for ever—a matter of meditation for ever. It is rather a thing of ugliness that is strictly a joy for ever.

All Dickens's books are Christmas books. But this is still truest of his two or three famous Yuletide tales— *The Christmas Carol* and *The Chimes* and *The Cricket on the Hearth*. Of these *The Christmas Carol* is beyond comparison the best as well as the most popular. Indeed, Dickens is in so profound and spiritual a sense a popular author that in his case, unlike most others, it can generally be said that the best work is the most popular. It is for *Pickwick* that he is best known; and upon the whole it is for Pickwick that he is best worth knowing. In any case this superiority of *The Christmas Carol* makes it convenient for us to take it as an example of the generalisations already made. If we study the very real atmosphere of rejoicing and of riotous charity in *The Christmas Carol* we shall find

that all the three marks I have mentioned are unmistakably visible. *The Christmas Carol* is a happy story
first, because it describes an abrupt and dramatic
change. It is not only the story of a conversion, but of
a sudden conversion; as sudden as the conversion of a
man at a Salvation Army meeting. Popular religion
is quite right in insisting on the fact of a crisis in most
things. It is true that the man at the Salvation
Army meeting would probably be converted from the
punch bowl; whereas Scrooge was converted to it.
That only means that Scrooge and Dickens represented
a higher and more historic Christianity.

Again, *The Christmas Carol* owes much of its hilarity
to our second source—the fact of its being a tale of
winter and of a very wintry winter. There is much
about comfort in the story; yet the comfort is never
enervating: it is saved from that by a tingle of something bitter and bracing in the weather. Lastly, the
story exemplifies throughout the power of the third principle—the kinship between gaiety and the grotesque.
Everybody is happy because nobody is dignified.
We have a feeling somehow that Scrooge looked even
uglier when he was kind than he had looked when he
was cruel. The turkey that Scrooge bought was so
fat, says Dickens, that it could never have stood
upright. That top-heavy and monstrous bird is a
good symbol of the top-heavy happiness of the
stories.

It is less profitable to criticise the other two tales in
detail because they represent variations on the theme in
two directions; and variations that were not, upon the
whole, improvements. *The Chimes* is a monument of

Dickens's honourable quality of pugnacity. He could not admire anything, even peace, without wanting to be warlike about it. That was all as it should be.

and the same thing done... (for literature)... different... Chatto...

DOMBEY AND SON

IN Dickens's literary life *Dombey and Son* represents a break so important as to necessitate our casting back to a summary and a generalisation. In order fully to understand what this break is, we must say something of the previous character of Dickens's novels, and even something of the general character of novels in themselves. How essential this is we shall see shortly.

It must first be remembered that the novel is the most typical of modern forms. It is typical of modern forms especially in this, that it is essentially formless. All the ancient modes or structures of literature were definite and severe. Any one composing them had to abide by their rules; they were what their name implied. Thus a tragedy might be a bad tragedy, but it was always a tragedy. Thus an epic might be a bad epic, but it was always an epic. Now in the sense in which there is such a thing as an epic, in that sense there is no such thing as a novel. We call any long fictitious narrative in prose a novel, just as we call any short piece of prose without any narrative an essay. Both these forms are really quite formless, and both of them are really quite new. The difference between a good epic by Mr. John Milton and a bad epic by Mr. John Smith was simply the difference between the same thing done

well and the same thing done badly. But it was not
(for instance) like the difference between *Clarissa
Harlowe* and *The Time Machine*. If we class Richard-
son's book with Mr. Wells's book it is really only for
convenience; if we say that they are both novels we
shall certainly be puzzled in that case to say what on
earth a novel is. But the note of our age, both for
good and evil, is a highly poetical and largely illogical
faith in liberty. Liberty is not a negation or a piece
of nonsense, as the cheap reactionaries say; it is a
belief in variety and growth. But it is a purely poetic
and even a merely romantic belief. The nineteenth
century was an age of romance as certainly as the
Middle Ages was an age of reason. Mediævals liked
to have everything defined and defensible; the modern
world prefers to run some risks for the sake of spon-
tancity and diversity. Consequently the modern world
is full of a phenomenon peculiar to itself—I mean the
spectacle of small or originally small things swollen to
enormous size and power. The modern world is like
a world in which toadstools should be as big as trees,
and insects should walk about in the sun as large as
elephants. Thus, for instance, the shopkeeper, almost
an unimportant figure in carefully ordered states, has
in our time become the millionaire, and has more power
than ten kings. Thus again a practical knowledge of
nature, of the habits of animals or the properties of
fire and water, was in the old ordered state either an
almost servile labour or a sort of joke; it was left to
old women and gamekeepers and boys who went
birds'-nesting. In our time this commonplace daily
knowledge has swollen into the enormous miracle of

physical size, weighing the stars and talking under the
sea. In short, our age is a sort of splendid jungle in
which some of the most towering weeds and blossoms
have come from the smallest seed.

And this is, generally speaking, the explanation of
the novel. The novel is not so much the filling up of an
artistic plan, however new or fantastic. It is a thing
that has grown from some germ of suggestion, and has
often turned out much larger than the author intended.
And this, lastly, is the final result of these facts, that
the critic can generally trace in a novel what was the
original artistic type or shape of thought from which
the whole matter started, and he will generally find
that this is different in every case. In one novel he
will find that the first impulse is a character. In another novel he will find that the first impulse is a
landscape, the atmosphere of some special countryside.
In another novel he will find that the first impulse is
the last chapter. Or it may be a thrust with sword or
dagger, it may be a theology, it may be a song. Somewhere embedded in every ordinary book are the five
or six words for which really all the rest will be written.
Some of our enterprising editors who set their readers to
hunt for banknotes and missing ladies might start a
competition for finding those words in every novel.
But whether or no this is possible, there is no doubt
that the principle in question is of great importance
in the case of Dickens, and especially in the case of
Dombey and Son.

In all the Dickens novels can be seen, so to speak, the
original thing that they were before they were novels.
The same may be observed, for the matter of that, in

the great novels of most of the great modern novelists. For example, Sir Walter Scott wrote poetical romances before he wrote prose romances. Hence it follows that, with all their much greater merit, his novels may still be described as poetical romances in prose. While adding a new and powerful element of popular humours and observation, Scott still retains a certain purely poetical right—a right to make his heroes and outlaws and great kings speak at the great moments with a rhetoric so rhythmical that it partakes of the nature of song, the same quite metrical rhetoric which is used in the metrical speeches of Marmion or Roderick Dhu. In the same way, although *Don Quixote* is a modern novel in its irony and subtlety, we can see that it comes from the old long romances of chivalry. In the same way, although *Clarissa* is a modern novel in its intimacy and actuality, we can see that it comes from the old polite letter-writing and polite essays of the period of the *Spectator*. Any one can see that Scott formed in *The Lay of the Last Minstrel* the style that he applied again and again afterwards, like the reappearances of a star taking leave of the stage. All his other romances were positively last appearances of the positively last Minstrel. Any one can see that Thackeray formed in fragmentary satires like *The Book of Snobs* or *The Yellowplush Papers* the style, the rather fragmentary style, in which he was to write *Vanity Fair*. In most modern cases, in short (until very lately, at any rate), the novel is an enormous outgrowth from something that was not a novel. And in Dickens this is very important. All his novels are outgrowths of the original notion of taking notes, splendid and

inspired notes, of what happens in the street.   Those
in the modern world who cannot reconcile themselves
to his method—those who feel that there is about his
books something intolerably clumsy or superficial—
have either no natural taste for strong literature at all,
or else have fallen into their error by too persistently
regarding Dickens as a modern novelist and expecting
all his books to be modern novels.   Dickens did not
know at what exact point he really turned into a novelist.   Nor do we.   Dickens did not know, in his deepest
soul, whether he ever really did turn into a novelist.
Nor do we.   The novel being a modern product is one
of the few things to which we really can apply that dis-
gusting method of thought—the method of evolution.
But even in evolution there are great gaps, there are
great breaks, there are great crises.   I have said that
the first of these breaks in Dickens may be placed at the
point when he wrote *Nicholas Nickleby*.   This was
his first serious decision to be a novelist in any sense at
all, to be anything except a maker of momentary
farces.   The second break, and that a far more important break, is in *Dombey and Son*.   This marks his
final resolution to be a novelist and nothing else, to be
a serious constructor of fiction in the serious sense.
Before *Dombey and Son* even his pathos had been really
frivolous.   After *Dombey and Son* even his absurdity
was intentional and grave.

In case this transition is not understood, one or two
tests may be taken at random.   The episodes in
Dombey and Son, the episodes in *David Copperfield*,
which came after it, are no longer episodes merely
stuck into the middle of the story without any connec-

tion with it, like most of the episodes in *Nicholas Nickleby*, or most of the episodes even in *Martin Chuzzlewit*. Take, for instance, by way of a mere coincidence, the fact that three schools for boys are described successively in *Nicholas Nickleby*, in *Dombey and Son*, and in *David Copperfield*. But the difference is enormous. Dotheboys Hall does not exist to tell us anything about Nicholas Nickleby. Rather Nicholas Nickleby exists entirely in order to tell us about Dotheboys Hall. It does not in any way affect his history or psychology; he enters Mr. Squeers's school and leaves Mr. Squeers's school with the same character, or rather absence of character. It is a mere episode, existing for itself. But when little Paul Dombey goes to an old-fashioned but kindly school, it is in a very different sense and for a very different reason from that for which Nicholas Nickleby goes to an old-fashioned and cruel school. The sending of little Paul to Dr. Blimber's is a real part of the history of little Paul, such as it is. Dickens deliberately invents all that elderly pedantry in order to show up Paul's childishness. Dickens deliberately invents all that rather heavy kindness in order to show up Paul's predestination and tragedy. Dotheboys Hall is not meant to show up anything except Dotheboys Hall. But although Dickens doubtless enjoyed Dr. Blimber quite as much as Mr. Squeers, it remains true that Dr. Blimber is really a very good foil to Paul; whereas Squeers is not a foil to Nicholas; Nicholas is merely a lame excuse for Squeers. The change can be seen continued in the school, or rather the two schools, to which David Copperfield goes. The whole idea of David Copperfield's life

is that he had the dregs of life before the wine of it.
He knew the worst of the world before he knew the
best of it. His childhood at Dr. Strong's is a second
childhood. Now for this purpose the two schools are
perfectly well adapted. Mr. Creakle's school is not
only, like Mr. Squeers's school, a bad school, it is a bad
influence upon David Copperfield. Dr. Strong's school
is not only a good school, it is a good influence upon
David Copperfield. I have taken this case of the
schools as a case casual but concrete. The same, however, can be seen in any of the groups or incidents of
the novels on both sides of the boundary. Mr. Crummles's theatrical company is only a society that Nicholas happens to fall into. America is only a place to
which Martin Chuzzlewit happens to go. These things
are isolated sketches, and nothing else. Even Todgers's
boarding-house is only a place where Mr. Pecksniff
can be delightfully hypocritical. It is not a place which
throws any new light on Mr. Pecksniff's hypocrisy.
But the case is different with that more subtle hypocrite
in *Dombey and Son*—I mean Major Bagstock. Dickens
does mean it as a deliberate light on Mr. Dombey's
character that he basks with a fatuous calm in the blazing sun of Major Bagstock's tropical and offensive
flattery. Here, then, is the essence of the change. He
not only wishes to write a novel; this he did as early
as *Nicholas Nickleby*. He wishes to have as little as
possible in the novel that does not really assist
it as a novel. Previously he had asked with the
assistance of what incidents could his hero wander
farther and farther from the pathway. Now he
has really begun to ask with the assistance of what

incidents his hero can get nearer and nearer to the goal.

The change made Dickens a greater novelist. I am not sure that it made him a greater man. One good character by Dickens requires all eternity to stretch its legs in; and the characters in his later books are always being tripped up by some tiresome nonsense about the story. For instance, in *Dombey and Son*, Mrs. Skewton is really very funny. But nobody with a love of the real smell of Dickens would compare her for a moment, for instance, with Mrs. Nickleby. And the reason of Mrs. Skewton's inferiority is simply this, that she has something to do in the plot; she has to entrap or assist to entrap Mr. Dombey into marrying Edith. Mrs. Nickleby, on the other hand, has nothing at all to do in the story, except to get in everybody's way. The consequence is that we complain not of her for getting in everyone's way, but of everyone for getting in hers. What are suns and stars, what are times and seasons, what is the mere universe, that it should presume to interrupt Mrs. Nickleby? Mrs. Skewton (though supposed, of course, to be a much viler sort of woman) has something of the same quality of splendid and startling irrelevancy. In her also there is the same feeling of wild threads hung from world to world like the webs of gigantic spiders; of things connected that seem to have no connection save by this one adventurous filament of frail and daring folly. Nothing could be better than Mrs. Skewton when she finds herself, after convolutions of speech, somehow on the subject of Henry VIII., and pauses to mention with approval "his dear little peepy eyes and his benevolent chin."

Nothing could be better than her attempt at Mahome-
dan resignation when she feels almost inclined to say
"that there is no What's-his-name but Thingummy,
and What-you-may-call-it is his prophet!" But she
has not so much time as Mrs. Nickleby to say these
good things; also she has not sufficient human virtue
to say them constantly. She is always intent upon
her worldly plans, among other things upon the worldly
plan of assisting Charles Dickens to get a story finished.
She is always "advancing her shrivelled ear" to listen
to what Dombey is saying to Edith. Worldliness is the
most solemn thing in the world; it is far more solemn
than other-worldliness. Mrs. Nickleby can afford to
ramble as a child does in a field, or as a child does to
laugh at nothing, for she is like a child, innocent. It is
only the good who can afford to be frivolous.

Broadly speaking, what is said here of Mrs. Skewton
applies to the great part of *Dombey and Son*, even to the
comic part of it. It shows an advance in art and unity;
it does not show an advance in genius and creation.
In some cases, in fact, I cannot help feeling that it
shows a falling off. It may be a personal idiosyncrasy,
but there is only one comic character really prominent
in Dickens, upon whom Dickens has really lavished
the wealth of his invention, and who does not amuse
me at all, and that character is Captain Cuttle. But
three great exceptions must be made to any such dis-
paragement of *Dombey and Son*. They are all three
of that royal order in Dickens's creation which can no
more be described or criticised than strong wine. The
first is Major Bagstock, the second is Cousin Feenix,
the third is Toots. In Bagstock Dickens has blasted

for ever that type which pretends to be sincere by the simple operation of being explosively obvious. He tells about a quarter of the truth, and then poses as truthful because a quarter of the truth is much simpler than the whole of it. He is the kind of man who goes about with posers for Bishops or for Socialists, with plain questions to which he wants a plain answer. His questions are plain only in the same sense that he himself is plain—in the sense of being uncommonly ugly. He is the man who always bursts with satisfaction because he can call a spade a spade, as if there were any kind of logical or philosophical use in merely saying the same word twice over. He is the man who wants things down in black and white, as if black and white were the only two colours; as if blue and green and red and gold were not facts of the universe. He is too selfish to tell the truth and too impatient even to hear it. He cannot endure the truth, because it is subtle. This man is almost always like Bagstock—a sycophant and a toad-eater. A man is not any the less a toad-eater because he eats his toads with a huge appetite and gobbles them up, as Bagstock did his breakfast, with the eyes starting out of his purple face. He flatters brutally. He cringes with a swagger. And men of the world like Dombey are always taken in by him, because men of the world are probably the simplest of all the children of Adam.

Cousin Feenix again is an exquisite suggestion, with his rickety chivalry and rambling compliments. It was about the period of *Dombey and Son* that Dickens began to be taken up by good society. (One can use only vulgar terms for an essentially vulgar process.)

And his sketches of the man of good family in the books of this period show that he had had glimpses of what that singular world is like. The aristocrats in his earliest books are simply dragons and griffins for his heroes to fight with—monsters like Sir Mulberry Hawk or Lord Verisopht. They are merely created upon the old principle, that your scoundrel must be polite and powerful—a very sound principle. The villain must be not only a villain, but a tyrant. The giant must be larger than Jack. But in the books of the Dombey period we have many shrewd glimpses of the queer realities of English aristocracy. Of these Cousin Feenix is one of the best. Cousin Feenix is a much better sketch of the essentially decent and chivalrous aristocrat than Sir Leicester Dedlock. Both of the men are, if you will, fools, as both are honourable gentlemen. But if one may attempt a classification among fools, Sir Leicester Dedlock is a stupid fool, while Cousin Feenix is a silly fool—which is much better. The difference is that the silly fool has a folly which is always on the borderland of wit, and even of wisdom; his wandering wits come often upon undiscovered truths. The stupid fool is as consistent and as homogeneous as wood; he is as invincible as the ancestral darkness. Cousin Feenix is a good sketch of the sort of well-bred old ass who is so fundamentally genuine that he is always saying very true things by accident. His whole tone also, though exaggerated like everything in Dickens, is very true to the bewildered good nature which marks English aristocratic life. The statement that Dickens could not describe a gentleman is, like most popular animadversions against

Dickens, so very thin and one-sided a truth as to be for serious purposes a falsehood. When people say that Dickens could not describe a gentleman, what they mean is this, and so far what they mean is true. They mean that Dickens could not describe a gentleman as gentlemen feel a gentleman. They mean that he could not take that atmosphere easily, accept it as the normal atmosphere, or describe that world from the inside. This is true. In Dickens's time there was such a thing as the English people, and Dickens belonged to it. Because there is no such thing as an English people now, almost all literary men drift towards what is called Society; almost all literary men either are gentlemen or pretend to be. Hence, as I say, when we talk of describing a gentleman, we always mean describing a gentleman from the point of view of one who either belongs to, or is interested in perpetuating, that type. Dickens did not describe gentlemen in the way that gentlemen describe gentlemen. He described them in the way in which he described waiters, or railway guards, or men drawing with chalk on the pavement. He described them, in short (and this we may freely concede), from the outside, as he described any other oddity or special trade. But when it comes to saying that he did not describe them well, then that is quite another matter, and that I should emphatically deny. The things that are really odd about the English upper class he saw with startling promptitude and penetration, and if the English upper class does not see these odd things in itself, it is not because they are not there, but because we are all blind to our own oddities; it is for the same reason that tramps do not feel dirty, or

that niggers do not feel black.   I have often heard a
dear old English oligarch say that Dickens could not
describe a gentleman, while every note of his own voice
and turn of his own hand recalled Sir Leicester Dedlock.
I have often been told by some old buck that Dickens
could not describe a gentleman, and been told so in the
shaky voice and with all the vague allusiveness of
Cousin Feenix.

Cousin Feenix has really many of the main points
of the class that governs England. Take, for an
instance, his hazy notion that he is in a world where
everybody knows everybody; whenever he mentions
a man, it is a man "with whom my friend Dombey is
no doubt acquainted." That pierces to the very
helpless soul of aristocracy. Take again the stupen-
dous gravity with which he leads up to a joke. That
is the very soul of the House of Commons and the
Cabinet, of the high-class English politics, where a
joke is always enjoyed solemnly. Take his insistence
upon the technique of Parliament, his regrets for the
time when the rules of debate were perhaps better
observed than they are now. Take that wonderful
mixture in him (which is the real human virtue of our
aristocracy) of a fair amount of personal modesty with
an innocent assumption of rank. Of a man who saw
all these genteel foibles so clearly it is absurd merely to
say without further explanation that he could not
describe a gentleman. Let us confine ourselves to
saying that he did not describe a gentleman as gentlemen like to be described.

Lastly, there is the admirable study of Toots, who
may be considered as being in some ways the master-

piece of Dickens. Nowhere else did Dickens express with such astonishing insight and truth his main contention, which is that to be good and idiotic is not a poor fate, but, on the contrary, an experience of primeval innocence, which wonders at all things. Dickens did not know, anymore than any great man ever knows, what was the particular thing that he had to preach. He did not know it; he only preached it. But the particular thing that he had to preach was this: That humility is the only possible basis of enjoyment; that if one has no other way of being humble except being poor, then it is better to be poor, and to enjoy; that if one has no other way of being humble except being imbecile, then it is better to be imbecile, and to enjoy. That is the deep unconscious truth in the character of Toots—that all his externals are flashy and false; all his internals unconscious, obscure, and true. He wears loud clothes, and he is silent inside them. His shirts and waistcoats are covered with bright spots of pink and purple, while his soul is always covered with the sacred shame. He always gets all the outside things of life wrong, and all the inside things right. He always admires the right Christian people, and gives them the wrong Christian names. Dimly connecting Captain Cuttle with the shop of Mr. Solomon Gills, he always addresses the astonished mariner as "Captain Gills." He turns Mr. Walter Gay, by a most improving transformation, into "Lieutenant Walters." But he always knows which people upon his own principles to admire. He forgets who they are, but he remembers what they are. With the clear eyes of humility he perceives the whole world as it is.

He respects the Game Chicken for being strong, as even the Game Chicken ought to be respected for being strong. He respects Florence for being good, as even Florence ought to be respected for being good. And he has no doubt about which he admires most; he prefers goodness to strength, as do all masculine men. It is through the eyes of such characters as Toots that Dickens really sees the whole of his tales. For even if one calls him a half-wit, it still makes a difference that he keeps the right half of his wits. When we think of the unclean and craven spirit in which Toots might be treated in a psychological novel of to-day; how he might walk with a mooncalf face, and a brain of bestial darkness, the soul rises in real homage to Dickens for showing how much simple gratitude and happiness can remain in the lopped roots of the most simplified intelligence. If scientists must treat a man as a dog, it need not be always as a mad dog. They might grant him, like Toots, a little of the dog's loyalty and the dog's reward.

DAVID COPPERFIELD

In this book Dickens is really trying to write a new kind of book, and the enterprise is almost as chivalrous as a cavalry charge. He is making a romantic attempt to be realistic. That is almost the definition of *David Copperfield*. In his last book, *Dombey and Son*, we see a certain maturity and even a certain mild exhaustion in his earlier farcical method. He never failed to have fine things in any of his books, and Toots is a very fine thing. Still, I could never find Captain Cuttle and Mr. Sol Gills very funny, and the whole Wooden Midshipman seems to me very wooden. In *David Copperfield* he suddenly unseals a new torrent of truth, the truth out of his own life. The impulse of the thing is autobiography; he is trying to tell all the absurd things that have happened to himself, and not the least absurd thing is himself. Yet though it is Dickens's ablest and clearest book, there is in it a falling away of a somewhat singular kind.

Generally speaking there was astonishingly little of fatigue in Dickens's books. He sometimes wrote bad work; he sometimes wrote even unimportant work; but he wrote hardly a line which is not full of his own fierce vitality and fancy. If he is dull it is hardly ever because he cannot think of anything; it is because, by some silly excitement or momentary lapse of judgment, he has thought of something that was not worth thinking of. If his joke is feeble, it is as an impromptu joke at an uproarious dinner-table may be feeble; it is no indication of any lack of vitality. The joke is feeble, but it is not a sign of feebleness. Broadly speaking, this is true of Dickens. If his writing is not amusing us, at least it is amusing him. Even when he is tiring he is not tired.

But in the case of *David Copperfield* there is a real reason for noting an air of fatigue. For although this is the best of all Dickens's books, it constantly disappoints the critical and intelligent reader. The reason is that Dickens began it under his sudden emotional impulse of telling the whole truth about himself and gradually allowed the whole truth to be more and more diluted, until towards the end of the book we are back in the old pedantic and decorative art of Dickens, an art which we justly admired in its own place and on its own terms, but which we resent when we feel it gradually returning through a tale pitched originally in a more practical and piercing key. Here, I say, is the one real example of the fatigue of Dickens. He begins his story in a new style and then slips back into an old one. The earlier part is in his later manner. The later part is in his earlier manner.

There are many marks of something weak and shadowy in the end of *David Copperfield*. Here, for instance, is one of them which is not without its bearing on many tendencies of modern England. Why did Dickens at the end of this book give way to that typically English optimism about emigration? He seems to think that he can cure the souls of a whole

cartload, or rather boatload, of his characters by sending them all to the Colonies. Peggotty is a desolate and
insulted parent whose house has been desecrated and his
pride laid low; therefore let him go to Australia. Emily
is a woman whose heart is broken and whose honour is
blasted; but she will be quite happy if she goes to
Australia. Mr. Micawber is a man whose soul cannot
be made to understand the tyranny of time or the limits
of human hope; but he will understand all these things
if he goes to Australia. For it must be noted that
Dickens does not use this emigration merely as a mode
of exit. He does not send these characters away on a
ship merely as a symbol suggesting that they pass
wholly out of his hearer's life. He does definitely
suggest that Australia is a sort of island Valley of
Avalon, where the soul may heal it of its grievous
wound. It is seriously suggested that Peggotty finds
peace in Australia. It is really indicated that Emily
regains her dignity in Australia. It is positively
explained of Mr. Micawber not that he was happy in
Australia (for he would be that anywhere), but that
he was definitely prosperous and practically successful
in Australia; and that he would certainly be nowhere.
Colonising is not talked of merely as a coarse, economic
expedient for going to a new market. It is really
offered as something that will cure the hopeless tragedy
of Peggotty; as something that will cure the still more
hopeless comedy of Micawber.

I will not dwell here on the subsequent adventures
of this very sentimental and extremely English illusion.
It would be an exaggeration to say that Dickens in
this matter is something of a forerunner of much

modern imperialism.   His political views were such
that he would have regarded modern imperialism with
horror and contempt.   Nevertheless there is here something of that hazy sentimentalism which makes some
Imperialists prefer to talk of the fringe of the empire
of which they know nothing, rather than of the heart
of the empire which they know is diseased.   It is
said that in the twilight and decline of Rome, close to
the dark ages, the people in Gaul believed that Britain
was a land of ghosts (perhaps it was foggy), and that
the dead were ferried across to it from the northern
coast of France.   If (as is not entirely impossible) our
own century appears to future ages as a time of temporary decay and twilight, it may be said that there
was attached to England a blessed island called Australia to which the souls of the socially dead were
ferried across to remain in bliss for ever.

This element which is represented by the colonial
optimism at the end of *David Copperfield* is a moral
element.   The truth is that there is something a little
mean about this sort of optimism.   I do not like the
notion of David Copperfield sitting down comfortably
to his tea-table with Agnes, having got rid of all the
inconvenient or distressing characters of the story by
sending them to the other side of the world.   The whole
thing has too much about it of the selfishness of a
family which sends a scapegrace to the Colonies to
starve with its blessing.   There is too much in the
whole thing of that element which was satirised by
an ironic interpretation of the epitaph "Peace, perfect
peace, with loved ones far away."   We should have
thought more of David Copperfield (and also of Charles

Dickens) if he had endeavoured for the rest of his life, by conversation and comfort, to bind up the wounds of his old friends from the seaside. We should have thought more of David Copperfield (and also of Charles Dickens) if he had faced the possibility of going on till his dying day lending money to Mr. Wilkins Micawber. We should have thought more of David Copperfield (and also of Charles Dickens) if he had not looked upon the marriage with Dora merely as a flirtation, an episode which he survived and ought to survive. And yet the truth is that there is nowhere in fiction where we feel so keenly the primary human instinct and principle that a marriage is a marriage and irrevocable, that such things do leave a wound and also a bond as in this case of David's short connection with his silly little wife. When all is said and done, when Dickens has done his best and his worst, when he has sentimentalised for pages and tried to tie up everything in the pink tape of optimism, the fact, in the psychology of the reader, still remains. The reader does still feel that David's marriage to Dora was a real marriage; and that his marriage to Agnes was nothing, a middle-aged compromise, a taking of the second best, a sort of spiritualised and sublimated marriage of convenience. For all the readers of Dickens Dora is thoroughly avenged. The modern world (intent on anarchy in everything, even in Government) refuses to perceive the permanent element of tragic constancy which inheres in all passion, and which is the origin of marriage. Marriage rests upon the fact that you cannot have your cake and eat it; that you cannot lose your heart and have it. But, as I have said, there is perhaps no place

in literature where we feel more vividly the sense of
this monogamous instinct in man than in David
Copperfield. A man is monogamous even if he is only
monogamous for a month; love is eternal even if it is
only eternal for a month. It always leaves behind it
the sense of something broken and betrayed.

But I have mentioned Dora in this connection only
because she illustrates the same fact which Micawber
illustrates; the fact that there is at the end of this book
too much tendency to bless people and get rid of them.
Micawber is a nuisance. Dickens the despot condemns
him to exile. Dora is a nuisance. Dickens the despot
condemns her to death. But it is the whole business
of Dickens in the world to express the fact that such
people are the spice and interest of life. It is the whole
point of Dickens that there is nobody more worth
living with than a strong, splendid, entertaining, immortal nuisance. Micawber interrupts practical life;
but what is practical life that it should venture to interrupt Micawber? Dora confuses the housekeeping;
but we are not angry with Dora because she confuses
the housekeeping. We are angry with the housekeeping because it confuses Dora. I repeat, and it cannot be too much repeated that the whole lesson of
Dickens is here. It is better to know Micawber than
not to know the minor worries that arise out of knowing Micawber. It is better to have a bad debt and a
good friend. In the same way it is better to marry
a human and healthy personality which happens to
attract you than to marry a mere housewife; for a mere
housewife is a mere housekeeper. All this was what
Dickens stood for; that the very people who are most

irritating in small business circumstances are often the people who are most delightful in long stretches of experience of life. It is just the man who is maddening when he is ordering a cutlet or arranging an appointment who is probably the man in whose company it is worth while to journey steadily towards the grave. Distribute the dignified people and the capable people and the highly business-like people among all the situations which their ambition or their innate corruption may demand; but keep close to your heart, keep deep in your inner councils the absurd people. Let the clever people pretend to govern you, let the unimpeachable people pretend to advise you, but let the fools alone influence you; let the laughable people whose faults you see and understand be the only people who are really inside your life, who really come near you or accompany you on your lonely march towards the last impossibility. That is the whole meaning of Dickens; that we should keep the absurd people for our friends. And here at the end of *David Copperfield* he seems in some dim way to deny it. He seems to want to get rid of the preposterous people simply because they will always continue to be preposterous. I have a horrible feeling that David Copperfield will send even his aunt to Australia if she worries him too much about donkeys.

I repeat, then, that this wrong ending of *David Copperfield* is one of the very few examples in Dickens of a real symptom of fatigue. Having created splendid beings for whom alone life might be worth living, he cannot endure the thought of his hero living with them. Having given his hero superb and terrible

friends, he is afraid of the awful and tempestuous vista
of their friendship. He slips back into a more superficial kind of story and ends it in a more superficial way.
He is afraid of the things he has made; of that terrible
figure Micawber; of that yet more terrible figure Dora.
He cannot make up his mind to see his hero perpetually
entangled in the splendid tortures and sacred surprises
that come from living with really individual and un-
manageable people. He cannot endure the idea that
his fairy prince will not have henceforward a perfectly
peaceful time. But the wise old fairy tales (which are
the wisest things in the world, at any rate the wisest
things of worldly origin), the wise old fairy tales never
were so silly as to say that the prince and the princess
lived peacefully ever afterwards. The fairy tales said
that the prince and princess lived happily ever afterwards: and so they did. They lived happily, although
it is very likely that from time to time they threw the
furniture at each other. Most marriages, I think,
are happy marriages; but there is no such thing as a
contented marriage. The whole pleasure of marriage
is that it is a perpetual crisis. David Copperfield and
Dora quarrelled over the cold mutton; and if they had
gone on quarrelling to the end of their lives, they would
have gone on loving each other to the end of their lives;
it would have been a human marriage. But David
Copperfield and Agnes would agree about the cold
mutton. And that cold mutton would be very cold.

I have here endeavoured to suggest some of the main
merits of Dickens within the framework of one of his
faults. I have said that *David Copperfield* represents a
rather sad transition from his strongest method to his

weakest. Nobody would ever complain of Charles
Dickens going on writing his own kind of novels, his
old kind of novels. If there be anywhere a man who
loves good books, that man wishes that there were four
Oliver Twists and at least forty-four *Pickwicks*. If
there be any one who loves laughter and creation, he
would be glad to read a hundred of *Nicholas Nickleby*
and two hundred of *The Old Curiosity Shop*. But
while any one would have welcomed one of Dickens's
own ordered and conventional novels, it was not in
this spirit that they welcomed *David Copperfield*.

David Copperfield begins as if it were going to be a
new kind of Dickens novel; then it gradually turns into
an old kind of Dickens novel. It is here that many
readers of this splendid book have been subtly and
secretly irritated. Nicholas Nickleby is all very well;
we accept him as something which is required to tie
the whole affair together. Nicholas is a sort of string
or clothes-line on which are hung the limp figure of
Smike, the jumping-jack of Mr. Squeers and the twin
dolls named Cheeryble. If we do not accept Nicholas
Nickleby as the hero of the story, at least we accept
him as the title of the story. But in *David Copperfield*
Dickens begins something which looks for the moment
fresh and startling. In the earlier chapters (the
amazing earlier chapters of this book) he does seem to be
going to tell the living truth about a living boy and man.
It is melancholy to see that sudden fire fading. It is
sad to see David Copperfield gradually turning into
Nicholas Nickleby. Nicholas Nickleby does not exist
at all; he is a quite colourless primary condition of
the story. We look through Nicholas Nickleby at the

story just as we look through a plain pane of glass at the
street.   But David Copperfield does begin by existing;
it is only gradually that he gives up that exhausting
habit.

Any fair critical account of Dickens must always
make him out much smaller than he is.   For any fair
criticism of Dickens must take account of his evident
errors, as I have taken account of one of the most
evident of them during the last two or three pages.
It would not even be loyal to conceal them.   But no
honest criticism, no criticism, though it spoke with
the tongues of men and angels, could ever really talk
about Dickens.   In all this that I have said I have not
been talking about Dickens at all.   I say it with equa-
nimity; I say it even with arrogance.   I have been talking about the gaps of Dickens.   I have been talking
about the omissions of Dickens.   I have been talking
about the slumber of Dickens and the forgetfulness and
unconsciousness of Dickens.   In one word, I have been
talking not about Dickens, but about the absence of
Dickens.   But when we come to him and his work
itself, what is there to be said?   What is there to be
said about earthquake and the dawn?   He has created,
especially in this book of *David Copperfield*, he has
created, creatures who cling to us and tyrannise over
us, creatures whom we would not forget if we could,
creatures whom we could not forget if we would,
creatures who are more actual than the man who
made them.

This is the excuse for all that indeterminate and rambling and sometimes sentimental criticism of which
Dickens, more than any one else, is the victim, of

which I fear that I for one have made him the victim in this place. When I was a boy I could not understand why the Dickensians worried so wearily about Dickens, about where he went to school and where he ate his dinners, about how he wore his trousers and when he cut his hair. I used to wonder why they did not write something that I could read about a man like Micawber. But I have come to the conclusion that this almost hysterical worship of the man, combined with a comparatively feeble criticism on his works, is just and natural. Dickens was a man like ourselves; we can see where he went wrong, and study him without being stunned or getting the sunstroke. But Micawber is not a man; Micawber is the superman. We can only walk round and round him wondering what we shall say. All the critics of Dickens, when all is said and done, have only walked round and round Micawber wondering what they should say. I am myself at this moment walking round and round Micawber wondering what I shall say. And I have not found out yet.

CHRISTMAS STORIES

THE power of Dickens is shown even in the scraps of Dickens, just as the virtue of a saint is said to be shown in fragments of his property or rags from his robe. It is with such fragments that we are chiefly concerned in the *Christmas Stories*. Many of them are fragments in the literal sense; Dickens began them and then allowed some one else to carry them on; they are almost rejected notes. In all the other cases we have been considering the books that he wrote; here we have rather to consider the books that he might have written. And here we find the final evidence and the unconscious stamp of greatness, as we might find it in some broken bust or some rejected moulding in the studio of Michael Angelo.

These sketches or parts of sketches all belong to that period in his later life when he had undertaken the duties of an editor, the very heavy duties of a very popular editor. He was not by any means naturally fitted for that position. He was the best man in the world for founding papers; but many people wished that he could have been buried under the foundations, like the first builder in some pagan and prehistoric pile. He called the *Daily News* into existence, but when once it existed, it objected to him strongly. It is not easy, and perhaps it is not important, to state truly the cause of this incapacity. It was not in the least what is called the ordinary fault or weakness of the artist. It was not that he was careless; rather it was that he was too conscientious. It was not that he had the irresponsibility of genius; rather it was that he had the irritating responsibility of genius; he wanted everybody to see things as he saw them. But in spite of all this he certainly ran two great popular periodicals—*Household Words* and *All the Year Round*—with enormous popular success. And he certainly so far succeeded in throwing himself into the communism of journalism, into the nameless brotherhood of a big paper, that many earnest Dickensians are still engaged in picking out pieces of Dickens from the anonymous pages of *Household Words* and *All the Year Round*, and those parts which have been already beyond question picked out and proved are often fragmentary. The genuine writing of Dickens breaks off at a certain point, and the writing of some one else begins. But when the writing of Dickens breaks off, I fancy that we know it.

The singular thing is that some of the best work that Dickens ever did, better than the work in his best novels, can be found in these slight and composite scraps of journalism. For instance, the solemn and self-satisfied account of the duty and dignity of a waiter given in the opening chapter of *Somebody's Luggage* is quite as full and fine as anything done anywhere by its author in the same vein of sumptuous satire. It is as good as the account which Mr. Bumble gives of out-door relief, which, "properly understood, is the parochial safeguard. The great thing is to give the paupers what they don't want, and then they never come again." It is as good as Mr. Podsnap's description of the British Constitution, which was bestowed on him by Providence. None of these celebrated passages is more obviously Dickens at his best than this, the admirable description of "the true principles of waitering," or the account of how the waiter's father came back to his mother in broad daylight, "in itself an act of madness on the part of a waiter," and how he expired repeating continually "two and six is three and four is nine." That waiter's explanatory soliloquy might easily have opened an excellent novel, as *Martin Chuzzlewit* is opened by the clever nonsense about the genealogy of the Chuzzlewits, or as *Bleak House* is opened by a satiric account of the damp, dim life of a law court. Yet Dickens practically abandoned the scheme of *Somebody's Luggage;* he only wrote two sketches out of those obviously intended. He may almost be said to have only written a brilliant introduction to another man's book.

Yet it is exactly in such broken outbreaks that his greatness appears. If a man has flung away bad ideas he has shown his sense, but if he has flung away good ideas he has shown his genius. He has proved that he actually has that over-pressure of pure creativeness which we see in nature itself, "that of a hundred seeds, she often brings but one to bear." Dickens had to be Malthusian about his spiritual children. Critics have called Keats and others who died young "the great Might-have-beens of literary history." Dickens certainly was not merely a great Might-have-been. Dickens, to say the least of him, was a great Was.

Yet this fails fully to express the richness of his talent;
for the truth is that he was a great Was and also a
great Might-have-been. He said what he had to say,
and yet not all he had to say. Wild pictures, possible
stories, tantalising and attractive trains of thought,
perspectives of adventure, crowded so continually upon
his mind that at the end there was a vast mass of them
left over, ideas that he literally had not the opportunity
to develop, tales that he literally had not the time to
tell. This is shown clearly in his private notes and
letters, which are full of schemes singularly striking
and suggestive, schemes which he never carried out.
It is indicated even more clearly by these *Christmas
Stories*, collected out of the chaotic opulence of *Household Words* and *All the Year Round*. He wrote short
stories actually because he had not time to write long
stories. He often put into the short story a deep and
branching idea which would have done very well for a
long story; many of his long stories, so to speak, broke
off short. This is where he differs from most who are
called the Might-have-beens of literature. Marlowe
and Chatterton failed because of their weakness.
Dickens failed because of his force.

Examine for example this case of the waiter in
Somebody's Luggage. Dickens obviously knew enough
about that waiter to have made him a running spring
of joy throughout a whole novel; as the beadle is in
Oliver Twist, or the undertaker in *Martin Chuzzlewit*.
Every touch of him tingles with truth, from the vague
gallantry with which he asks, "Would'st thou know,
fair reader (if of the adorable female sex)" to the official
severity with which he takes the chambermaid down,

"as many pegs as is desirable for the future comfort of all parties." If Dickens had developed this character at full length in a book he would have preserved for ever in literature a type of great humour and great value, and a type which may only too soon be disappearing from English history. He would have eternalised the English waiter. He still exists in some sound old taverns and decent country inns, but there is no one left really capable of singing his praises. I know that Mr. Bernard Shaw has done something of the sort in the delightfully whimsical account of William in *You Never Can Tell*. But nothing will persuade me that Mr. Bernard Shaw can really understand the English waiter. He can never have ordered wine from him for instance. And though the English waiter is by the nature of things solemn about everything, he can never reach the true height and ecstasy of his solemnity except about wine. What the real English waiter would do or say if Mr. Shaw asked him for a vegetarian meal I cannot dare to predict. I rather think that for the first time in his life he would laugh— a horrible sight.

Dickens's waiter is described by one who is not merely witty, truthful, and observant, like Mr. Bernard Shaw, but one who really knew the atmosphere of inns, one who knew and even liked the smell of beef, and beer, and brandy. Hence there is a richness in Dickens's portrait which does not exist in Mr. Shaw's. Mr. Shaw's waiter is merely a man of tact; Dickens's is a man of principle. Mr. Shaw's waiter is an opportunist, just as Mr. Shaw is an opportunist in politics. Dickens's waiter is ready to stand up seriously for "the true principles of waitering," just as Dickens was ready to stand up for the true principles of Liberalism. Mr. Shaw's waiter is agnostic; his motto is "You never can tell." Dickens's waiter is a dogmatist; his motto is "You can tell; I will tell you." And the true old-fashioned English waiter had really this grave and even moral attitude; he was the servant of the customers as a priest is the servant of the faithful, but scarcely in any less dignified sense. Surely it is not mere patriotic partiality that makes one lament the disappearance of this careful and honourable figure crowded out by meaner men at meaner wages, by the German waiter who has learnt five languages in the course of running away from his own, or the Italian waiter who regards those he serves with a darkling contempt which must certainly be that either of a dynamiter or an exiled prince. The human and hospitable English waiter is vanishing. And Dickens might perhaps have saved him, as he saved Christmas.

I have taken this case of the waiter in Dickens and his equally important counterpart in England as an example of the sincere and genial sketches scattered about these short stories. But there are many others, and one at least demands special mention; I mean Mrs. Lirriper, the London landlady. Not only did Dickens never do anything better in a literary sense, but he never performed more perfectly his main moral function, that of insisting through laughter and flippancy upon the virtue of Christian charity. There has been much broad farce against the lodging-house keeper: he alone could have written broad farce in her favour. It is fashionable to represent the landlady as a tyrant;

it is too much forgotten that if she is one of the oppressors she is at least as much one of the oppressed. If she is bad-tempered it is often for the same reasons that make all women bad-tempered (I suppose the exasperating qualities of the other sex); if she is grasping it is often because when a husband makes generosity a vice it is often necessary that a wife should make avarice a virtue. All this Dickens suggested very soundly and in a few strokes in the more remote character of Miss Wozenham. But in Mrs. Lirriper he went further and did not fare worse. In Mrs. Lirriper he suggested quite truly how huge a mass of real good humour, of grand unconscious patience, of unfailing courtesy and constant and difficult benevolence is concealed behind many a lodging-house door and compact in the red-faced person of many a preposterous landlady. Any one could easily excuse the ill-humour of the poor. But great masses of the poor have not even any ill-humour to be excused. Their cheeriness is startling enough to be the foundation of a miracle play; and certainly is startling enough to be the foundation of a romance. Yet I do not know of any romance in which it is expressed except this one.

Of the landlady as of the waiter it may be said that Dickens left in a slight sketch what he might have developed through a long and strong novel. For Dickens had hold of one great truth, the neglect of which has, as it were, truncated and made meagre the work of many brilliant modern novelists. Modern novelists try to make long novels out of subtle characters. But a subtle character soon comes to an end, because it works in and in to its own centre and dies there. But a

simple character goes on for ever in a fresh interest
and energy, because it works out and out into the
infinite universe. Mr. George Moore in France is not
by any means so interesting as Mrs. Lirriper in France;
for she is trying to find France and he is only trying
to find George Moore. Mrs. Lirriper is the female
equivalent of Mr. Pickwick. Unlike Mrs. Bardell
(another and lesser landlady) she was fully worthy to
be Mrs. Pickwick. For in both cases the essential
truth is the same; that original innocence which alone
deserves adventures and because it alone can appreciate
them. We have had Mr. Pickwick in England and
we can imagine him in France. We have had Mrs.
Lirriper in France and we can imagine her in Mesopo-
tamia or in heaven. The subtle character in the
modern novels we cannot really imagine anywhere
except in the suburbs or in Limbo.

BLEAK HOUSE

Bleak House is not certainly Dickens's best book; but perhaps it is his best novel. Such a distinction is not a mere verbal trick; it has to be remembered rather constantly in connection with his work. This particular story represents the highest point of his intellectual maturity. Maturity does not necessarily mean perfection. It is idle to say that a mature potato is perfect; some people like new potatoes. A mature potato is not perfect, but it is a mature potato; the mind of an intelligent epicure may find it less adapted to his particular purpose; but the mind of an intelligent potato would at once admit it as being, beyond all doubt, a genuine, fully developed specimen of his own particular species. The same is in some degree true even of literature. We can say more or less when a human being has come to his full mental growth, even if we go so far as to wish that he had never come to it. Children are very much nicer than grown-up people; but there is such a thing as growing up. When Dickens wrote *Bleak House* he had grown up.

Like Napoleon, he had made his army on the march. He had walked in front of his mob of aggressive characters as Napoleon did in front of the half-baked battalions of the Revolution. And, like Napoleon, he won battle after battle before he knew his own plan of campaign; like Napoleon, he put the enemies' forces to rout before he had put his own force into order Like Napoleon, he had a victorious army almost before he had an army. After his decisive victories Napoleon began to put his house in order; after his decisive victories Dickens also began to put his house in order. The house, when he had put it in order, was *Bleak House*.

There was one thing common to nearly all the other Dickens tales, with the possible exception of *Dombey and Son*. They were all rambling tales; and they all had a perfect right to be. They were all rambling tales for the very simple reason that they were all about rambling people. They were novels of adventure; they were even diaries of travel. Since the hero strayed from place to place, it did not seem unreasonable that the story should stray from subject to subject. This is true of the bulk of the novels up to and including *David Copperfield*, up to the very brink or threshold of *Bleak House*. Mr. Pickwick wanders about on the white English roads, always looking for antiquities and always finding novelties. Poor Oliver Twist wanders along the same white roads to seek his fortune and to find his misfortune. Nicholas Nickleby goes walking across England because he is young and hopeful; Little Nell's grandfather does the same thing because he is old and silly. There is not much in common between Samuel Pickwick and Oliver Twist; there is not much in common between Oliver Twist and Nicholas Nickleby; there is not much in common (let us hope) between Little Nell's grandfather and any other human being. But they all have this in common, that they may actually all have trodden in each other's footprints.

They were all wanderers on the face of the same fair
English land. *Martin Chuzzlewit* was only made popular
by the travels of the hero in America. When we come
to *Dombey and Son* we find, as I have said, an exception; but even here it is odd to note the fact that it
was an exception almost by accident. In Dickens's
original scheme of the story, much greater prominence
was to have been given to the travels and trials of
Walter Gay; in fact, the young man was to have had a
deterioration of character which could only have been
adequately detailed in him in his character of a
vagabond and a wastrel. The most important point,
however, is that when we come to *David Copperfield*,
in some sense the summit of his serious literature, we
find the thing still there. The hero still wanders from
place to place, his genius is still gipsy. The adventures
in the book are less violent and less improbable than
those which wait for Pickwick and Nicholas Nickleby;
but they are still adventures and not merely events;
they are still things met on a road. The facts of the
story fall away from David as such facts do fall away
from a traveller walking fast. We are more likely
perhaps, to pass by Mr. Creakle's school than to pass
by Mrs. Jarley's wax-works. The only point is that
we should pass by both of them. Up to this point
in Dickens's development, his novel, however true, is
still picaresque; his hero never really rests anywhere
in the story. No one seems really to know where Mr.
Pickwick lived. Here he has no abiding city.

When we come to *Bleak House*, we come to a change
in artistic structure. The thing is no longer a string of
incidents; it is a cycle of incidents. It returns upon

itself; it has recurrent melody and poetic justice; it
has artistic constancy and artistic revenge. It preserves
the unities; even to some extent it preserves the
unities of time and place. The story circles round two
or three symbolic places; it does not go straggling
irregularly all over England like one of Mr. Pickwick's
coaches. People go from one place to another place;
but not from one place to another place on the road to
everywhere else. Mr. Jarndyce goes from Bleak House
to visit Mr. Boythorn; but he comes back to Bleak
House. Miss Clare and Miss Summerson go from
Bleak House to visit Mr. and Mrs. Bayham Badger;
but they come back to Bleak House. The whole
story strays from Bleak House and plunges into the
foul fogs of Chancery and the autumn mists of Chesney
Wold; but the whole story comes back to Bleak House.
The domestic title is appropriate; it is a permanent
address.

Dickens's openings are almost always good; but the
opening of *Bleak House* is good in a quite new and striking sense. Nothing could be better, for instance, than
the first foolish chapter about the genealogy of the
Chuzzlewits; but it has nothing to do with the Chuzzlewits. Nothing could be better than the first chapter
of *David Copperfield;* the breezy entrance and banging
exit of Miss Betsy Trotwood. But if there is ultimately
any crisis or serious subject-matter of *David Copperfield*,
it is the marred marriage with Dora, the final return to
Agnes; and all this is in no way involved in the highly-
amusing fact that his aunt expected him to be a girl.
We may repeat that the matter is picaresque. The
story begins in one place and ends in another place,

and there is no real connection between the beginning
and the end except a biographical connection.

A picaresque novel is only a very eventful biography;
but the opening of *Bleak House* is quite another business altogether.   It is admirable in quite another way.
The description of the fog in the first chapter of *Bleak
House* is good in itself; but it is not merely good in itself,
like the description of the wind in the opening of *Martin
Chuzzlewit;* it is also good in the sense that Maeterlinck
is good; it is what the modern people call an atmosphere.   Dickens begins in the Chancery fog because
he means to end in the Chancery fog.   He did not begin in the Chuzzlewit wind because he meant to end in
it; he began in it because it was a good beginning.   This
is perhaps the best short way of stating the peculiarity
of the position of *Bleak House*.   In this *Bleak House*
beginning we have the feeling that it is not only a
beginning; we have the feeling that the author sees
the conclusion and the whole.   The beginning is alpha
and omega: the beginning and the end.   He means that
all the characters and all the events shall be read
through the smoky colours of that sinister and unnatural vapour.

The same is true throughout the whole tale; the
whole tale is symbolic and crowded with symbols.
Miss Flite is a funny character, like Miss La Creevy,
but Miss La Creevy means only Miss La Creevy.
Miss Flite means Chancery.   The rag-and-bone man,
Krook, is a powerful grotesque; so is Quilp; but in the
story Quilp only means Quilp; Krook means Chancery.
Rick Carstone is a kind and tragic figure, like Sidney
Carton; but Sidney Carton only means the tragedy of

human nature; Rick Carstone means the tragedy of
Chancery. Little Jo dies pathetically like Little Paul;
but for the death of Little Paul we can only blame Dickens; for the death of Little Jo we blame Chancery.
Thus the artistic unity of the book, compared to all
the author's earlier novels, is satisfying, almost suffocat-
ing. There is the *motif*, and again the *motif*. Almost
everything is calculated to assert and re-assert the
savage morality of Dickens's protest against a particular
social evil. The whole theme is that which another
Englishman as jovial as Dickens defined shortly and
finally as the law's delay. The fog of the first chapter
never lifts.

In this twilight he traced wonderful shapes. Those
people who fancy that Dickens was a mere clown; that
he could not describe anything delicate or deadly in
the human character,—those who fancy this are mostly
people whose position is explicable in many easy ways.
The vast majority of the fastidious critics have, in the
quite strict and solid sense of the words, never read
Dickens at all; hence their opposition is due to and
inspired by a hearty innocence which will certainly
make them enthusiastic Dickensians if they ever, by
some accident, happen to read him. In other cases
it is due to a certain habit of reading books under the
eye of a conventional critic, admiring what we expect
to admire, regretting what we are told to regret, waiting for Mr. Bumble to admire him, waiting for Little
Nell to despise her. Yet again, of course, it is sometimes due to that basest of all artistic indulgences
(certainly far baser than the pleasure of absinthe or
the pleasure of opium), the pleasure of appreciating

works of art which ordinary men cannot appreciate. Surely the vilest point of human vanity is exactly that; to ask to be admired for admiring what your admirers do not admire. But whatever be the reason, whether rude or subtle, which has prevented any particular man from personally admiring Dickens, there is in connection with a book like *Bleak House* something that may be called a solid and impressive challenge. Let anyone who thinks that Dickens could not describe the semi-tones and the abrupt instincts of real human nature simply take the trouble to read the stretch of chapters which detail the way in which Carstone's mind grew gradually morbid about his chances in Chancery. Let him note the manner in which the mere masculinity of Carstone is caught; how as he grows more mad he grows more logical, nay, more rational. Good women who love him come to him, and point out the fact that Jarndyce is a good man, a fact to them solid like an object of the senses. In answer he asks them to understand his position. He does not say this; he does not say that. He only urges that Jarndyce may have become cynical in the affair in the same sense that he himself may have become cynical in the affair. He is always a man; that is to say, he is always unanswerable, always wrong. The passionate certainty of the woman beats itself like battering waves against the thin smooth wall of his insane consistency. I repeat: let any one who thinks that Dickens was a gross and indelicate artist read that part of the book. If Dickens had been the clumsy journalist that such people represent, he never could have written such an episode at all. A clumsy journalist would have made

Rick Carstone in his mad career cast off Esther and Ada and the others. The great artist knew better. He knew that even if all the good in a man is dying, the last sense that dies is the sense that knows a good woman from a bad; it is like the scent of a noble hound.

The clumsy journalist would have made Rick Carstone turn on John Jarndyce with an explosion of hatred, as of one who had made an exposure—who had found out what low people call "a false friend" in what they call "his true colours." The great artist knew better; he knew that a good man going wrong tries to salve his soul to the last with the sense of generosity and intellectual justice. He will try to love his enemy if only out of mere love of himself. As the wolf dies fighting, the good man gone wrong dies arguing. This is what constitutes the true and real tragedy of Richard Carstone. It is strictly the one and only great tragedy that Dickens wrote. It is like the tragedy of Hamlet. The others are not tragedies because they deal almost with dead men. The tragedy of old Dorrit is merely the sad spectacle of a dotard dragged about Europe in his last childhood. The tragedy of Steerforth is only that of one who dies suddenly; the tragedy of old Dombey only that of one who was dead all the time. But Rick is a real tragedy, for he is still alive when the quicksand sucks him down.

It is impossible to avoid putting in the first place this pall of smoke which Dickens has deliberately spread over the story. It is quite true that the country underneath is clear enough to contain any number of unconscious comedians or of merry monsters such as he was in the custom of introducing into the carnival of his tales. But he meant us to take the smoky atmosphere seriously. Charles Dickens, who was, like all men who are really funny about funny things, horribly serious about serious things, certainly meant us to read this story in terms of his protest and his insurrection against the emptiness and arrogance of law, against the folly and the pride of judges. Everything else that there is in this story entered into it through the unconscious or accidental energy of his genius, which broke in at every gap. But it was the tragedy of Richard Carstone that he meant, not the comedy of Harold Skimpole. He could not help being amusing; but he meant to be depressing.

Another case might be taken as testing the greater seriousness of this tale. The passages about Mrs. Jellyby and her philanthropic schemes show Dickens at his best in his old and more familiar satiric manner. But in the midst of the Jellyby pandemonium, which is in itself described with the same *abandon* and irrelevance as the boarding-house of Mrs. Todgers or the travelling theatre of Mr. Crummles, the elder Dickens introduced another piece of pure truth and even tenderness. I mean the account of Caddy Jellyby. If Carstone is a truly masculine study of how a man goes wrong, Caddy is a perfectly feminine study of how a girl goes right. Nowhere else perhaps in fiction, and certainly nowhere else in Dickens, is the mere female paradox so well epitomised, the unjust use of words covering so much capacity for a justice of ultimate estimate; the seeming irresponsibility in language concealing such a fixed and pitiless sense of responsibil-

ity about things; the air of being always at daggers-
drawn with her own kindred, yet the confession of incurable kinship implied in pride and shame; and, above
all, that thirst for order and beauty as for something
physical; that strange female power of hating ugliness
and waste as good men can only hate sin and bad men
virtue. Every touch in her is true, from her first
bewildering outbursts of hating people because she
likes them, down to the sudden quietude and good sense
which announces that she has slipped into her natural
place as a woman. Miss Clare is a figure-head, Miss
Summerson in some ways a failure; but Miss Caddy
Jellyby is by far the greatest, the most human, and
the most really dignified of all the heroines of Dickens.

With one or two exceptions, all the effects in this
story are of this somewhat quieter kind, though none
of them are so subtly successful as Rick Carstone and
Caddy. Harold Skimpole begins as a sketch drawn
with a pencil almost as airy and fanciful as his own.
The humour of the earlier scenes is delightful—the
scenes in which Skimpole looks on at other people
paying his debts with the air of a kindly outsider, and
suggests in formless legal phraseology that they might
"sign something" or "make over something," or the
scene in which he tries to explain the advantages of
accepting everything to the apoplectic Mr. Boythorn.
But it was one of the defects of Dickens as a novelist
that his characters always became coarser and clumsier
as they passed through the practical events of a story,
and this would necessarily be so with Skimpole, whose
position was conceivable even to himself only on the
assumption that he was a mere spectator of life.

Poor Skimpole only asked to be kept out of the business of this world, and Dickens ought to have kept him out of the business of *Bleak House*. By the end of the tale he has brought Skimpole to doing acts of mere low villainy. This altogether spoils the ironical daintiness of the original notion. Skimpole was meant to end with a note of interrogation. As it is, he ends with a big, black, unmistakable blot. Speaking purely artistically, we may say that this is as great a collapse or vulgarisation as if Richard Carstone had turned into a common blackguard and wife-beater, or Caddy Jellyby into a comic and illiterate landlady. Upon the whole it may, I think, be said that the character of Skimpole is rather a piece of brilliant moralising than of pure observation or creation. Dickens had a singularly just mind. He was wild in his caricatures, but very sane in his impressions. Many of his books were devoted, and this book is partly devoted, to a denunciation of aristocracy—of the idle class that lives easily upon the toil of nations. But he was fairer than many modern revolutionists, and he insisted on satirising also those who prey on society not in the name of rank or law, but in the name of intellect and beauty. Sir Leicester Dedlock and Mr. Harold Skimpole are alike in accepting with a royal unconsciousness the anomaly and evil of their position. But the idleness and insolence of the aristocrat is human and humble compared to the idleness and insolence of the artist.

With the exception of a few fine freaks, such as Turveydrop and Chadband, all the figures in this book are touched more delicately, even more faintly, than is common with Dickens. But if the figures are touched more faintly, it is partly because they are figures in a fog—the fog of Chancery. Dickens meant that twilight to be oppressive; for it was the symbol of oppression. Deliberately he did not dispel the darkness at the end of this book, as he does dispel it at the end of most of his books. Pickwick gets out of the Fleet Prison; Carstone never gets out of Chancery but by death. This tyranny, Dickens said, shall not be lifted by the light subterfuge of a fiction. This tyranny shall never be lifted till all Englishmen lift it together.

CHILD'S HISTORY OF ENGLAND

THERE are works of great authors manifestly inferior to their typical work which are yet necessary to their fame and their figure in the world. It is not difficult to recall examples of them. No one, for instance, would talk of Scott's *Tales of a Grandfather* as indicating the power that produced *Kenilworth* and *Guy Mannering*. Nevertheless, without this chance minor compilation we should not really have the key of Scott. Without this one insignificant book we should not see his significance. For the truth was that Scott loved history more than romance, because he was so constituted as to find it more romantic than romance. He preferred the deeds of Wallace and Douglas to those of Marmion and Ivanhoe. Therefore his garrulous gossip of old times, his rambles in dead centuries, give us the real material and impulse of all his work; they represent the quarry in which he dug and the food on which he fed. Almost alone among novelists Scott actually preferred those parts of his historical novels which he had not invented himself. He exults when he can boast in an eager note that he has stolen some saying from history. Thus *The Tales of a Grandfather*, though small, is in some sense the frame of all the Waverley novels. We realise that all Scott's novels are tales of a grandfather.

What has been said here about Scott might be said

in a less degree about Thackeray's *Four Georges*. Though standing higher among his works than *The Tales of a Grandfather* among Scott's they are not his works of genius; yet they seem in some way to surround, supplement, and explain such works. Without the *Four Georges* we should know less of the link that bound Thackeray to the beginning and to the end of the eighteenth century; thence we should have known less of Colonel Esmond and also less of Lord Steyne. To these two examples I have given of the slight historical experiments of two novelists a third has to be added. The third great master of English fiction whose glory fills the nineteenth century also produced a small experiment in the popularisation of history. It is separated from the other two partly by a great difference of merit but partly also by an utter difference of tone and outlook. We seem to hear it suddenly as in the first words spoken by a new voice, a voice gay, colloquial, and impatient. Scott and Thackeray were tenderly attached to the past; Dickens (in his consciousness at any rate) was impatient with everything, but especially impatient with the past.

A collection of the works of Dickens would be incomplete in an essential as well as a literal sense without his *Child's History of England*. It may not be important as a contribution to history, but it is important as a contribution to biography; as a contribution to the character and the career of the man who wrote it, a typical man of his time. That he had made no personal historical researches, that he had no special historical learning, that he had not had, in truth, even anything that could be called a good education, all this only accentuates not the merit but at least the importance of the book. For here we may read in plain popular language, written by a man whose genius for popular exposition has never been surpassed among men, a brief account of the origin and meaning of England as it seemed to the average Englishman of that age. When subtler views of our history, some more false and some more true than his, have become popular, or at least well known, when in the near future Carlylean or Catholic or Marxian views of history have spread themselves among the reading public, this book will always remain as a bright and brisk summary of the cock-sure, healthy-minded, essentially manly and essentially ungentlemanly view of history which characterised the Radicals of that particular Radical era. The history tells us nothing about the periods that it talks about; but it tells us a great deal about the period that it does not talk about; the period in which it was written. It is in no sense a history of England from the Roman invasion; but it is certainly one of the documents which will contribute to a history of England in the nineteenth century.

Of the actual nature of its philosophical and technical limitations it is, I suppose, unnecessary to speak. They all resolve themselves into one fault common in the modern world, and certainly characteristic of historians much more learned and pretentious than Dickens. That fault consists simply in ignoring or under-rating the variety of strange evils and unique dangers in the world. The Radicals of the nineteenth century were engaged, and most righteously engaged, in dealing with one particular problem of human

civilisation; they were shifting and apportioning more
equally a load of custom that had really become unmeaning, often accidental, and nearly always unfair.
Thus, for instance, a fierce and fighting penal code,
which had been perfectly natural when the robbers
were as strong as the Government, had become in
more ordered times nothing but a base and bloody
habit. Thus again Church powers and dues, which
had been human when every man felt the Church as
the best part of himself, were mere mean privileges
when the nation was full of sects and full of free-
thinkers. This clearing away of external symbols
that no longer symbolised anything was an honourable and needful work; but it was so difficult that to
the men engaged in it it blocked up the perspective
and filled the sky, so that they slid into a very natural
mental mistake which coloured all their views of history.
They supposed that this particular problem on which
they were engaged was the one problem upon which all
mankind had always been engaged. They got it into
their heads that breaking away from a dead past was
the perpetual process of humanity. The truth is
obviously that humanity has found itself in many
difficulties very different from that. Sometimes the
best business of an age is to resist some alien invasion;
sometimes to preach practical self-control in a world
too self-indulgent and diffused; sometimes to prevent
the growth in the State of great new private enter-
prises that would poison or oppress it. Above all it
may sometimes happen that the highest task of a
thinking citizen may be to do the exact opposite of
the work which the Radicals had to do. It may be his

highest duty to cling on to every scrap of the past that he can find, if he feels that the ground is giving way beneath him and sinking into mere savagery and for-getfulness of all human culture. This was exactly the position of all thinking men in what we call the dark ages, say from the sixth to the tenth century. The cheap progressive view of history can never make head or tail of that epoch; it was an epoch upside down. We think of the old things as barbaric and the new things as enlightened. In that age all the enlightened things were old; all the barbaric and brutally ignorant things were new and up to date. Republicanism was a fading legend; despotism was a new and successful experiment. Christianity was not only better than the clans that rebelled against it; Christianity was more rationalistic than they were. When men looked back they saw progress and reason; when they looked for-ward they saw shapeless tradition and tribal terror. Touching such an age it is obvious that all our modern terms describing reform or conservation are foolish and beside the mark. The Conservative was then the only possible reformer. If a man did not strengthen the remains of Roman order and the root of Roman Christianity, he was simply helping the world to roll downhill into ruin and idiotcy. Remember all these evident historical truths and then turn to the account given by Charles Dickens of that great man, St. Dunstan. It is not that the pert cockney tone of the abuse is irritating to the nerves: it is that he has got the whole hang of the thing wrong. His head is full of the nineteenth-century situation; that a priest imposing discipline is a person somehow blocking the way to equality and light. Whereas the point about such a man as Dunstan was that nobody in the place except he cared a button about equality or light: and that he was defending what was left of them against the young and growing power of darkness and division and caste.

Nevertheless the case against such books as this is commonly stated wrong. The fault of Dickens is not (as is often said) that he "applies the same moral standard to all ages." Every sane man must do that: a moral standard must remain the same or it is not a moral standard. If we call St. Anthony of Padua a good man, we must mean what we mean when we call Huxley a good man, or else there is no sense in using the word "good." The fault of the Dickens school of popular history lies, not in the application of a plain rule of right and wrong to all circumstances, but in ignorance of the circumstances to which it was applied. It is not that they wrongly enforce the fixed principle that life should be saved; it is that they take a fire-engine to a shipwreck and a lifeboat to a house on fire. The business of a good man in Dickens's time was to bring justice up to date. The business of a good man in Dunstan's time was to toil to ensure the survival of any justice at all.

And Dickens, through being a living and fighting man of his own time, kept the health of his own heart, and so saw many truths with a single eye: truths that were spoilt for subtler eyes. He was much more really right than Carlyle; immeasurably more right than Froude. He was more right precisely because he applied plain human morals to all facts as he saw them.

Carlyle really had a vague idea that in coarse and cruel times it was right to be coarse and cruel; that tyranny was excusable in the twelfth century: as if the twelfth century did not denounce tyrants as much or more than any other. Carlyle, in fact, fancied that Rufus was the right sort of man; a view which was not only not shared by Anselm, but was probably not shared by Rufus. In this connection, or rather in connection with the other case of Froude, it is worth while to take another figure from Dickens's history, which illustrates the other and better side of the facile and popular method. Sheer ignorance of the environment made him wrong about Dunstan. But sheer instinct and good moral tradition made him right, for instance, about Henry VIII.; right where Froude is wildly wrong. Dickens's imagination could not re-picture an age where learning and liberty were dying rather than being born: but Henry VIII. lived in a time of expanding knowledge and unrest; a time therefore somewhat like the Victorian. And Dickens in his childish but robust way does perceive the main point about him: that he was a wicked man. He misses all the fine shades, of course; he makes him every kind of wicked man at once. He leaves out the serious interests of the man: his strange but real concern for theology; his love of certain legal and moral forms; his half-unconscious patriotism. But he sees the solid bulk of definite badness simply because it was there; and Froude cannot see it at all; because Froude followed Carlyle and played tricks with the eternal conscience. Henry VIII. *was* "a blot of blood and grease upon the history of England." For he was the embodiment of the

Devil in the Renascence, that wild worship of mere
pleasure and scorn, which with its pictures and its
palaces has enriched and ruined the world.

The time will soon come when the mere common-
sense of Dickens, like the mere common-sense of
Macaulay (though his was poisoned by learning and
Whig politics), will appear to give a plainer and therefore truer picture of the mass of history than the
mystical perversity of a man of genius writing only out
of his own temperament, like Carlyle or Taine. If a
man has a new theory of ethics there is one thing he
must not be allowed to do. Let him give laws on
Sinai, let him dictate a Bible, let him fill the world
with cathedrals if he can. But he must not be allowed
to write a history of England; or a history of any country. All history was conducted on ordinary morality:
with his extraordinary morality he is certain to read it
all askew. Thus Carlyle tries to write of the Middle
Ages with a bias against humility and mercy; that is,
with a bias against the whole theoretic morality of the
Middle Ages. The result is that he turns into a mere
turmoil of arrogant German savages what was really
the most complete and logical, if not the highest, of
human civilisations. Historically speaking, it is better
to be Dickens than to be this; better to be ignorant,
provincial, slap-dash, seeing only the passing moment,
but in that moment, to be true to eternal things.

It must be remembered, of course, that Dickens
deliberately offers this only as a "child's" history of
England. That is, he only professes to be able to
teach history as any father of a little boy of five professes to be able to teach him history. And although

the history of England would certainly be taught very differently (as regards the actual criticism of events and men) in a family with a wider culture or with another religion, the general method would be the same.   For the general method is quite right.   This black-and-white history of heroes and villains; this history full of pugnacious ethics and of nothing else, is the right kind of history for children.   I have often wondered how the scientific Marxians and the believers in "the materialist view of history" will ever manage to teach their dreary economic generalisations to children: but I suppose they will have no children.   Dickens's history will always be popular with the young; almost as popular as Dickens's novels, and for the same reason: because it is full of moralising.   Science and art without morality are not dangerous in the sense commonly supposed.   They are not dangerous like a fire, but dangerous like a fog.   A fire is dangerous in its brightness; a fog in its dulness; and thought without morals is merely dull, like a fog.   The fog seems to be creeping up the street; putting out lamp after lamp. But this cockney lamp-post which the children love is still crowned with its flame; and when the fathers have forgotten ethics, their babies will turn and teach them.

HARD TIMES

I HAVE heard that in some debating clubs there is a rule that the members may discuss anything except religion and politics. I cannot imagine what they do discuss; but it is quite evident that they have ruled out the only two subjects which are either important or amusing. The thing is a part of a certain modern tendency to avoid things because they lead to warmth; whereas, obviously, we ought, even in a social sense, to seek those things specially. The warmth of the discussion is as much a part of hospitality as the warmth of the fire. And it is singularly suggestive that in English literature the two things have died together. The very people who would blame Dickens for his sentimental hospitality are the very people who would also blame him for his narrow political conviction. The very people who would mock him for his narrow radicalism are those who would mock him for his broad fireside. Real conviction and real charity are much nearer than people suppose. Dickens was capable of loving all men; but he refused to love all opinions. The modern humanitarian can love all opinions, but he cannot love all men; he seems, sometimes, in the ecstasy of his humanitarianism, even to hate them all. He can love all opinions, including the opinion that men are unlovable.

In feeling Dickens as a lover we must never forget him as a fighter, and a fighter for a creed; but indeed there is no other kind of fighter. The geniality which he spread over all his creations was geniality spread from one centre, from one flaming peak. He was willing to excuse Mr. Micawber for being extravagant; but Dickens and Dickens's doctrine were strictly to decide how far he was to be excused. He was willing to like Mr. Twemlow in spite of his snobbishness, but Dickens and Dickens's doctrine were alone to be judges of how far he was snobbish. There was never a more didactic writer: hence there was never one more amusing. He had no mean modern notion of keeping the moral doubtful. He would have regarded this as a mere piece of slovenliness, like leaving the last page illegible.

Everywhere in Dickens's work these angles of his absolute opinion stood up out of the confusion of his general kindness, just as sharp and splintered peaks stand up out of the soft confusion of the forests. Dickens is always generous, he is generally kind-hearted, he is often sentimental, he is sometimes intolerably maudlin; but you never know when you will not come upon one of the convictions of Dickens; and when you do come upon it you do know it. It is as hard and as high as any precipice or peak of the mountains. The highest and hardest of these peaks is *Hard Times*.

It is here more than anywhere else that the sternness of Dickens emerges as separate from his softness; it is here, most obviously, so to speak, that his bones stick out. There are indeed many other books of his which are written better and written in a sadder tone. *Great Expectations* is melancholy in a sense; but it is doubtful of everything, even of its own melancholy. *The Tale of Two Cities* is a great tragedy, but it is still a sentimental tragedy. It is a great drama, but it is still a melodrama. But this tale of *Hard Times* is in some way harsher than all these. For it is the expression of a righteous indignation which cannot condescend to humour and which cannot even condescend to pathos. Twenty times we have taken Dickens's hand and it has been sometimes hot with revelry and sometimes weak with weariness; but this time we start a little, for it is inhumanly cold; and then we realise that we have touched his gauntlet of steel.

One cannot express the real value of this book without being irrelevant. It is true that one cannot express the real value of anything without being irrelevant. If we take a thing frivolously we can take it separately, but the moment we take a thing seriously, if it were only an old umbrella, it is obvious that that umbrella opens above us into the immensity of the whole universe. But there are rather particular reasons why the value of the book called *Hard Times* should be referred back to great historic and theoretic matters with which it may appear superficially to have little or nothing to do. The chief reason can perhaps be stated thus— that English politics had for more than a hundred years been getting into more and more of a hopeless tangle (a tangle which, of course, has since become even worse) and that Dickens did in some extraordinary way see what was wrong, even if he did not see what was right.

The Liberalism which Dickens and nearly all of his contemporaries professed had begun in the American and the French Revolutions. Almost all modern

English criticism upon those revolutions has been vitiated by the assumption that those revolutions burst upon a world which was unprepared for their ideas—a world ignorant of the possibility of such ideas. Somewhat the same mistake is made by those who suggest that Christianity was adopted by a world incapable of criticising it; whereas obviously it was adopted by a world that was tired of criticising everything. The vital mistake that is made about the French Revolution is merely this—that everyone talks about it as the introduction of a new idea. It was not the introduction of a new idea; there are no new ideas. Or if there are new ideas, they would not cause the least irritation if they were introduced into political society; because the world having never got used to them there would be no mass of men ready to fight for them at a moment's notice. That which was irritating about the French Revolution was this—that it was not the introduction of a new ideal, but the practical fulfilment of an old one. From the time of the first fairy tales men had always believed ideally in equality; they had always thought that something ought to be done, if anything could be done, to redress the balance between Cinderella and the ugly sisters. The irritating thing about the French was not that they said this ought to be done; everybody said that. The irritating thing about the French was that they did it. They proposed to carry out into a positive scheme what had been the vision of humanity; and humanity was naturally annoyed. The kings of Europe did not make war upon the Revolution because it was a blasphemy, but because it was a copy-book maxim which had been just too accurately copied. It was a platitude which they had always held in theory unexpectedly put into practice. The tyrants did not hate democracy because it was a paradox; they hated it because it was a truism which seemed in some danger of coming true.

Now it happens to be hugely important to have this right view of the Revolution in considering its political effects upon England. For the English, being a deeply and indeed excessively romantic people, could never be quite content with this quality of cold and bald obviousness about the republican formula. The republican formula was merely this—that the State must consist of its citizens ruling equally, however unequally they may do anything else. In their capacity of members of the State they are all equally interested in its preservation. But the English soon began to be romantically restless about this eternal truism; they were perpetually trying to turn it into something else, into something more picturesque—progress perhaps, or anarchy. At last they turned it into the highly exciting and highly unsound system of politics, which was known as the Manchester School, and which was expressed with a sort of logical flightiness, more excusable in literature, by Mr. Herbert Spencer. Of course Danton or Washington or any of the original republicans would have thought these people were mad. They would never have admitted for a moment that the State must not interfere with commerce or competition; they would merely have insisted that if the State did interfere, it must really be the State—that is, the whole people. But the distance between the common sense of Danton and the mere ecstasy of Herbert Spencer marks the English way of colouring and altering the revolutionary idea. The English people as a body went blind, as the saying is, for interpreting democracy entirely in terms of liberty. They said in substance that if they had more and more liberty it did not matter whether they had any equality or any fraternity. But this was violating the sacred trinity of true politics; they confounded the persons and they divided the substance.

Now the really odd thing about England in the nineteenth century is this—that there was one Englishman who happened to keep his head. The men who lost their heads lost highly scientific and philosophical heads; they were great cosmic systematisers like Spencer, great social philosophers like Bentham, great practical politicians like Bright, great political economists like Mill. The man who kept his head kept a head full of fantastic nonsense; he was a writer of rowdy farces, a demagogue of fiction, a man without education in any serious sense whatever, a man whose whole business was to turn ordinary cockneys into extraordinary caricatures. Yet when all these other children of the revolution went wrong he, by a mystical something in his bones, went right. He knew nothing of the Revolution; yet he struck the note of it. He returned to the original sentimental commonplace upon which it is forever founded, as the Church is founded on a rock. In an England gone mad about a minor theory he reasserted the original idea—the idea that no one in the State must be too weak to influence the State.

This man was Dickens. He did this work much more genuinely than it was done by Carlyle or Ruskin;

for they were simply Tories making out a romantic case for the return of Toryism. But Dickens was a real Liberal demanding the return of real Liberalism. Dickens was there to remind people that England had rubbed out two words of the revolutionary motto, had left only Liberty and destroyed Equality and Fraternity. In this book, *Hard Times*, he specially champions equality. In all his books he champions fraternity.

The atmosphere of this book and what it stands for can be very adequately conveyed in the note on the book by Lord Macaulay, who may stand as a very good example of the spirit of England in those years of eager emancipation and expanding wealth—the years in which Liberalism was turned from an omnipotent truth to a weak scientific system. Macaulay's private comment on *Hard Times* runs, "One or two passages of exquisite pathos and the rest sullen Socialism." That is not an unfair and certainly not a specially hostile criticism, but it exactly shows how the book struck those people who were mad on political liberty and dead about everything else. Macaulay mistook for a new formula called Socialism what was, in truth, only the old formula called political democracy. He and his Whigs had so thoroughly mauled and modified the original idea of Rousseau or Jefferson that when they saw it again they positively thought that it was something quite new and eccentric. But the truth was that Dickens was not a Socialist, but an unspoilt Liberal; he was not sullen; nay, rather, he had remained strangely hopeful. They called him a sullen Socialist only to disguise their astonishment at finding still loose about the London streets a happy republican.

Dickens is the one living link between the old kindness and the new, between the good will of the past and the good works of the future. He links May Day with Bank Holiday, and he does it almost alone. All the men around him, great and good as they were, were in comparison puritanical, and never so puritanical as when they were also atheistic. He is a sort of solitary pipe down which pours to the twentieth century the original river of Merry England. And although this *Hard Times* is, as its name implies, the hardest of his works, although there is less in it perhaps than in any of the others of the *abandon* and the buffoonery of Dickens, this only emphasises the more clearly the fact that he stood almost alone for a more humane and hilarious view of democracy. None of his great and much more highly-educated contemporaries could help him in this. Carlyle was as gloomy on the one side as Herbert Spencer on the other. He protested against the commercial oppression simply and solely because it was not only an oppression but a depression. And this protest of his was made specially in the case of the book before us. It may be bitter, but it was a protest against bitterness. It may be dark, but it is the darkness of the subject and not of the author. He is by his own account dealing with hard times, but not with a hard eternity, not with a hard philosophy of the universe. Nevertheless, this is the one place in his work where he does not make us remember human happiness by example as well as by precept. This is, as I have said, not the saddest, but certainly the harshest of his stories. It is perhaps the only place where Dickens, in defending happiness, for a moment forgets to be happy.

He describes Bounderby and Gradgrind with a degree of grimness and sombre hatred very different from the half affectionate derision which he directed against the old tyrants or humbugs of the earlier nineteenth century —the pompous Dedlock or the fatuous Nupkins, the grotesque Bumble or the inane Tigg. In those old books his very abuse was benignant; in *Hard Times* even his sympathy is hard. And the reason is again to be found in the political facts of the century. Dickens could be half genial with the older generation of oppressors because it was a dying generation. It was evident, or at least it seemed evident then, that Nupkins could not go on much longer making up the law of England to suit himself; that Sir Leicester Dedlock could not go on much longer being kind to his tenants as if they were dogs and cats. And some of these evils the nineteenth century did really eliminate or improve. For the first half of the century Dickens and all his friends were justified in feeling that the chains were falling from mankind. At any rate, the chains did fall from Mr. Rouncewell the Iron-master. And when they fell from him he picked them up and put them upon the poor.

LITTLE DORRIT

Little Dorrit stands in Dickens's life chiefly as a signal of how far he went down the road of realism, of sadness, and of what is called modernity. True, it was by no means the best of the books of his later period; some even think it the worst. *Great Expectations* is certainly the best of the later novels; some even think it the best of all the novels. Nor is it the novel most concerned with strictly recent problems; that title must be given to *Hard Times*. Nor again is it the most finely finished or well constructed of the later books; that claim can be probably made for *Edwin Drood*. By a queer verbal paradox the most carefully finished of his later tales is the tale that is not finished at all. In form, indeed, the book bears a superficial resemblance to those earlier works by which the young Dickens had set the whole world laughing long ago. Much of the story refers to a remote time early in the nineteenth century; much of it was actually recalled and copied from the life of Dickens's father in the old Marshalsea prison. Also the narrative has something of the form, or rather absence of form, which belonged to *Nicholas Nickleby* or *Martin Chuzzlewit*. It has something of the old air of being a string of disconnected adventures, like a boy's book about bears and Indians. The Dorrits go wandering for no particular reason on the Continent of Europe, just as young Martin Chuzzlewit went wandering for no particular reason on the continent of America. The story of *Little Dorrit* stops and lingers at the doors of the Circumlocution Office much in the same way that the story of Samuel Pickwick stops and lingers in the political excitement of Eatanswill. The villain, Blandois, is a very stagey villain indeed; quite as stagey as Ralph Nickleby or the mysterious Monk. The secret of the dark house of Clennam is a very silly secret; quite as silly as the secret of Ralph Nickleby or the secret of Monk. Yet all these external similarities between *Little Dorrit* and the earliest books, all this loose, melodramatic quality, only serves to make more obvious and startling the fact that some change has come over the soul of Dickens. *Hard Times* is harsh; but then *Hard Times* is a social pamphlet; perhaps it is only harsh as a social pamphlet must be harsh. *Bleak House* is a little sombre; but then *Bleak House* is almost a detective story; perhaps it is only sombre in the sense that a detective story must be sombre. *A Tale of Two Cities* is a tragedy; but then *A Tale of Two Cities* is a tale of the French Revolution; perhaps it is only a tragedy because the French Revolution was a tragedy. *The Mystery of Edwin Drood* is dark; but then the mystery of anybody must be dark. In all these other cases of the later books an artistic reason can be given—a reason of theme or of construction for the slight sadness that seems to cling to them. But exactly because *Little Dorrit* is a mere Dickens novel, it shows that something must somehow have happened to Dickens himself. Even in resuming his old liberty, he cannot resume his old hilarity. He can re-create the anarchy, but not the revelry.

It so happens that this strange difference between the new and the old mode of Dickens can be symbolised and stated in one separate and simple contrast. Dickens's father had been a prisoner in a debtors' prison, and Dickens's works contain two pictures partly suggested by the personality of that prisoner. Mr. Micawber is one picture of him. Mr. Dorrit is another. This truth is almost incredible, but it is the truth. The joyful Micawber, whose very despair was exultant, and the desolate Dorrit, whose very pride was pitiful, were the same man. The valiant Micawber and the nervous, shaking Dorrit were the same man. The defiant Micawber and the snobbish, essentially obsequious Dorrit were the same man. I do not mean of course that either of the pictures was an exact copy of anybody. The whole Dickens genius consisted of taking hints and turning them into human beings. As he took twenty real persons and turned them into one fictitious person, so he took one real person and turned him into twenty fictitious persons. This quality would suggest one character, that quality would suggest another. But in this case, at any rate, he did take one real person and turn him into two. And what is more, he turned him into two persons who seem to be quite opposite persons. To ordinary readers of Dickens, to say that Micawber and Dorrit had in any sense the same original, will appear unexpected and wild. No conceivable connection between the two would ever have occurred to anybody who had read Dickens with simple and superficial enjoyment, as all good literature ought to be read.

It will seem to them just as silly as saying that the Fat Boy and Mr. Alfred Jingle were both copied from the same character. It will seem as insane as saying that the character of Smike and the character of Major Bagstock were both copied from Dickens's father. Yet it is an unquestionable historical fact that Micawber and Dorrit were both copied from Dickens's father, in the only sense that any figures in good literature are ever copied from anything or anybody. Dickens did get the main idea of Micawber from his father; and that idea is that a poor man is not conquered by the world. And Dickens did get the main idea of Dorrit from his father; and that idea is that a poor man may be conquered by the world. I shall take the opportunity of discussing, in a moment, which of these ideas is true. Doubtless old John Dickens included both the gay and the sad moral; most men do. My only purpose here is to point out that Dickens drew the gay moral in 1849, and the sad moral in 1857.

There must have been some real sadness at this time creeping like a cloud over Dickens himself. It is nothing that a man dwells on the darkness of dark things; all healthy men do that. It is when he dwells on the darkness of bright things that we have reason to fear some disease of the emotions. There must really have been some depression when a man can only see the sad side of flowers or the sad side of holidays or the sad side of wine. And there must be some depression of an uncommonly dark and genuine character when a man has reached such a point that he can see only the sad side of Mr. Wilkins Micawber.

Yet this is in reality what had happened to Dickens

about this time. Staring at Wilkins Micawber he could see only the weakness and the tragedy that was made possible by his indifference, his indulgence, and his bravado. He had already indeed been slightly moved towards this study of the feebleness and ruin of the old epicurean type with which he had once sympathised, the type of Bob Sawyer or Dick Swiveller. He had already attacked the evil of it in *Bleak House* in the character of Harold Skimpole, with its essentially cowardly carelessness and its highly selfish communism. Nevertheless, as I have said before, it must have been no small degree of actual melancholia which led Dickens to look for a lesson of disaster and slavery in the very same career from which he had once taught lessons of continual recuperation and a kind of fantastic freedom. There must have been at this time some melancholy behind the writings. There must have existed on this earth at the time that portent and paradox—a somewhat depressed Dickens.

Perhaps it was a reminiscence of that metaphorical proverb which tells us that "truth lies at the bottom of a well." Perhaps these people thought that the only way to find truth in the well was to drown oneself. But on whatever thin theoretic basis, the type and period of George Gissing did certainly consider that Dickens, so far as he went, was all the worse for the optimism of the story of Micawber; hence it is not unnatural that they should think him all the better for the comparative pessimism of the story of *Little Dorrit*. The very things in the tale that would naturally displease the ordinary admirers of Dickens, are the things which would naturally please a man like George Gissing. There are many of these things, but one of them emerges pre-eminent and unmistakable. This is the fact that when all is said and done the main business of the story of *Little Dorrit* is to describe the victory of circumstances over a soul. The circumstances are the financial ruin and long imprisonment of Edward Dorrit; the soul is Edward Dorrit himself. Let it be granted that the circumstances are exceptional and oppressive, are denounced as exceptional and oppressive, are finally exploded and overthrown; still, they are circumstances. Let it be granted that the soul is that of a man perhaps weak in any case and retaining many merits to the last, still it is a soul. Let it be granted, above all, that the admission that such spiritual tragedies do occur does not decrease by so much as an iota our faith in the validity of any spiritual struggle. For example, Stevenson has made a study of the breakdown of a good man's character under a burden for which he is not to blame, in the tragedy of Henry Durie in *The Master of Ballantrae*. Yet he has added, in the mouth of Mackellar, the exact common sense and good theology of the matter, saying "It matters not a jot; for he that is to pass judgment upon the records of our life is the same that formed us in frailty." Let us concede then all this, and the fact remains that the study of the slow demoralisation of a man through mere misfortune was not a study congenial to Dickens, not in accordance with his original inspiration, not connected in any manner with the special thing that he had to say. In a word, the thing is not quite a part of himself; and he was not quite himself when he did it.

He was still quite a young man; his depression did not

come from age. In fact, as far as I know, mere depression never does come from mere age. Age can pass into a beautiful reverie. Age can pass into a sort of beautiful idiocy. But I do not think that the actual decline and close of our ordinary vitality brings with it any particular heaviness of the spirits. The spirits of the old do not as a rule seem to become more and more ponderous until they sink into the earth. Rather the spirits of the old seem to grow lighter and lighter until they float away like thistledown. Wherever there is the definite phenomenon called depression, it commonly means that something else has been closer to us than so normal a thing as death. There has been disease, bodily or mental, or there has been sin, or there has been some struggle or effort, breaking past the ordinary boundaries of human custom. In the case of Dickens there had been two things that are not of the routine of a wholesome human life; there had been the quarrel with his wife, and there had been the strain of incessant and exaggerated intellectual labour. He had not an easy time; and on top of that (or perhaps rather at the bottom of it) he had not an easy nature. Not only did his life necessitate work, but his character necessitated worry about work; and that combination is always one which is very dangerous to the temperament which is exposed to it. The only people who ought to be allowed to work are the people who are able to shirk. The only people who ought to be allowed to worry are the people who have nothing to worry about. When the two are combined, as they were in Dickens, you are very likely to have at least one collapse. *Little Dorrit* is a very interesting, sincere, and fascinating book. But for all that, I fancy it is the one collapse.

The complete proof of this depression may be difficult to advance; because it will be urged, and entirely with reason, that the actual examples of it are artistic and appropriate. Dickens, the Gissing school will say, was here pointing out certain sad truths of psychology; can any one say that he ought not to point them out? That may be; in any case, to explain depression is not to remove it. But the instances of this more sombre quality of which I have spoken are not very hard to find. The thing can easily be seen by comparing a book like *Little Dorrit* with a book like *David Copperfield*. David Copperfield and Arthur Clennam have both been brought up in unhappy homes, under bitter guardians and a black, disheartening religion. It is the whole point of David Copperfield that he has broken out of a Calvinistic tyranny which he cannot forgive. But it is the whole point of Arthur Clennam that he has not broken out of the Calvinistic tyranny, but is still under its shadow. Copperfield has come from a gloomy childhood; Clennam, though forty years old, is still in a gloomy childhood. When David meets the Murdstones again it is to defy them with the health and hilarious anger that go with his happy delirium about Dora. But when Clennam re-enters his sepulchral house there is a weight upon his soul which makes it impossible for him to answer, with any spirit, the morbidities of his mother, or even the grotesque interferences of Mr. Flintwinch. This is only another example of the same quality which makes the Dickens of *Little Dorrit* insist on the degradation of the debtor, while the Dickens of *David Copperfield* insisted on his splendid irresponsibility, his essential emancipation. Imprisonments passed over Micawber like summer clouds. But the imprisonment in *Little Dorrit* is like a complete natural climate and environment; it has positively modified the shapes and functions of the animals that dwell in it. A horrible thing has happened to Dickens; he has almost become an Evolutionist. Worse still, in studying the Calvinism of Mrs. Clennam's house, he has almost become a Calvinist. He half believes (as do some of the modern scientists) that there is really such a thing as "a child of wrath," that a man on whom such an early shadow had fallen could never shake it off. For ancient Calvinism and modern Evolutionism are essentially the same things. They are both ingenious logical blasphemies against the dignity and liberty of the human soul.

The workmanship of the book in detail is often extremely good. The one passage in the older and heartier Dickens manner (I mean the description of the Circumlocution Office) is beyond praise. It is a complete picture of the way England is actually governed at this moment. The very core of our politics is expressed in the light and easy young Barnacle who told Clennam with a kindly frankness that he, Clennam, would "never go on with it." Dickens hit the mark so that the bell rang when he made all the lower officials, who were cads, tell Clennam coldly that his claim was absurd, until the last official, who is a gentleman, tells him genially that the whole business is absurd. Even here, perhaps, there is something more than the old exuberant derision of Dickens; there is a touch of experience that verges on scepticism.

Everywhere else, certainly, there is the note which I have called Calvinistic; especially in the predestined passion of Tattycoram or the incurable cruelty of Miss Wade. Even Little Dorrit herself had, we are told, one stain from her prison experience; and it is spoken of like a bodily stain; like something that cannot be washed away.

There is no denying that this is Dickens's dark moment. It adds enormously to the value of his general view of life that such a dark moment came. He did what all the heroes and all the really happy men have done; he descended into Hell. Nor is it irreverent to continue the quotation from the Creed, for in the next book he was to write he was to break out of all these dreams of fate and failure, and with his highest voice to speak of the triumph of the weak of this world. His next book was to leave us saying, as Sydney Carton mounted the scaffold, words which, splendid in them-selves, have never been so splendidly quoted—"I am the Resurrection and the Life; whoso believeth in Me though he be dead yet he shall live." In Sydney Carton at least, Dickens shows none of that dreary submission to the environment of the irrevocable that had for an instant lain on him like a cloud. On this occasion he sees with the old heroic clearness that to be a failure may be one step to being a saint. On the third day he rose again from the dead.

A TALE OF TWO CITIES

As an example of Dickens's literary work, *A Tale of Two Cities* is not wrongly named. It is his most typical contact with the civic ideals of Europe. All his other tales have been tales of one city. He was in spirit a Cockney; though that title has been quite unreasonably twisted to mean a cad. By the old sound and proverbial test a Cockney was a man born within the sound of Bow bells. That is, he was a man born within the immediate appeal of high civilisation and of eternal religion. Shakespeare, in the heart of his fantastic forest, turns with a splendid suddenness to the Cockney ideal as being the true one after all. For a jest, for a reaction, for an idle summer love or still idler summer hatred, it is well to wander away into the bewildering forest of Arden. It is well that those who are sick with love or sick with the absence of love, those who weary of the folly of courts or weary yet more of their wisdom, it is natural that these should trail away into the twinkling twilight of the woods. Yet it is here that Shakespeare makes one of his most arresting and startling assertions of the truth. Here is one of those rare and tremendous moments of which one may say that there is a stage direction, "Enter Shakespeare." He has admitted that for men weary of courts, for men sick of cities, the wood is the wisest place, and he has praised it with his purest lyric ecstasy. But when a man enters suddenly upon that celestial picnic, a man who is not sick of cities, but sick of hunger, a man who is not weary of courts, but weary of walking, then Shakespeare lets through his own voice with a shattering sincerity and cries the praise of practical human civilisation:

> If ever you have looked on better days,
> If ever you have sat at good men's feasts,
> If ever been where bells have knolled to church,
> If ever from your eyelids wiped a tear
> Or know what 't is to pity and be pitied.

There is nothing finer even in Shakespeare than that conception of the circle of rich men all pretending to rough it in the country, and the one really hungry man entering, sword in hand, and praising the city. "If ever been where bells have knolled to church"; if you have ever been within sound of Bow bells; if you have ever been happy and haughty enough to call yourself a Cockney.

We must remember this distinction always in the case of Dickens. Dickens is the great Cockney, at once tragic and comic, who enters abruptly upon the Arcadian banquet of the æsthetics and says, "Forbear and eat no more," and tells them that they shall not eat "until necessity be served." If there was one thing he would have favoured instinctively it would have been the spreading of the town as meaning the spreading of civilisation. And we should (I hope) all favour the spreading of the town if it did mean the spreading of civilisation. The objection to the spread-

ing of the modern Manchester or Birmingham suburb
is simply that such a suburb is much more barbaric
than any village in Europe could ever conceivably be.
And again, if there is anything that Dickens would
have definitely hated it is that general treatment of
nature as a dramatic spectacle, a piece of scene-painting
which has become the common mark of the culture of
our wealthier classes.   Despite many fine pictures of
natural scenery, especially along the English road-
sides, he was upon the whole emphatically on the side
of the town.   He was on the side of bricks and mortar.
He was a citizen; and, after all, a citizen means a man of
the city.   His strength was, after all, in the fact that
he was a man of the city.   But, after all, his weakness,
his calamitous weakness, was that he was a man of one
city.

For all practical purposes he had never been outside
such places as Chatham and London.   He did indeed
travel on the Continent; but surely no man's travel was
ever so superficial as his.   He was more superficial than
the smallest and commonest tourist.   He went about
Europe on stilts; he never touched the ground.   There
is one good test and one only of whether a man has
travelled to any profit in Europe.   An Englishman is,
as such, a European, and as he approaches the central
splendours of Europe he ought to feel that he is coming
home.   If he does not feel at home he had much better have stopped at home.   England is a real home;
London is a real home; and all the essential feelings of
adventure or the picturesque can easily be gained by
going out at night upon the flats of Essex or the cloven
hills of Surrey.   Your visit to Europe is useless unless

it gives you the sense of an exile returning. Your first sight of Rome is futile unless you feel that you have seen it before. Thus useless and thus futile were the foreign experiments and the continental raids of Dickens. He enjoyed them as he would have enjoyed, as a boy, a scamper out of Chatham into some strange meadows, as he would have enjoyed, when a grown man, a steam in a police boat out into the fens to the far east of London. But he was the Cockney venturing far; he was not the European coming home. He is still the splendid Cockney Orlando of whom I spoke above; he cannot but suppose that any strange men, being happy in some pastoral way, are mysterious foreign scoundrels. Dickens's real speech to the lazy and laughing civilisation of Southern Europe would really have run in the Shakespearian words:

> but whoe'er you be
> Who in this desert inaccessible,
> Under the shade of melancholy boughs
> Lose and neglect the creeping hours of time.
> If ever you have looked on better things,
> If ever been where bells have knolled to church.

If, in short, you have ever had the advantage of being born within the sound of Bow bells. Dickens could not really conceive that there was any other city but his own.

It is necessary thus to insist that Dickens never understood the Continent, because only thus can we appreciate the really remarkable thing he did in *A Tale of Two Cities*. It is necessary to feel, first of all, the fact that to him London was the centre of the universe. He did not understand at all the real sense in which Paris is the capital of Europe. He had never realised that all roads lead to Rome. He had never felt (as an Englishman can feel) that he was an Athenian before he was a Londoner. Yet with everything against him he did this astonishing thing. He wrote a book about two cities, one of which he understood; the other he did not understand. And his description of the city he did not know is almost better than his description of the city he did know. This is the entrance of the unquestionable thing about Dickens; the thing called genius; the thing which every one has to talk about directly and distinctly because no one knows what it is. For a plain word (as for instance the word fool) always covers an infinite mystery.

A Tale of Two Cities is one of the more tragic tints of the later life of Dickens. It might be said that he grew sadder as he grew older; but this would be false, for two reasons. First, a man never or hardly ever does grow sad as he grows old; on the contrary, the most melancholy young lovers can be found forty years afterwards chuckling over their port wine. And second, Dickens never did grow old, even in a physical sense. What weariness did appear in him appeared in the prime of life; it was due not to age but to overwork, and his exaggerative way of doing everything. To call Dickens a victim of elderly disenchantment would be as absurd as to say the same of Keats. Such fatigue as there was, was due not to the slowing down of his blood, but rather to its unremitting rapidity. He was not wearied by his age; rather he was wearied by his youth. And though *A Tale of Two Cities* is full

of sadness, it is full also of enthusiasm; that pathos
is a young pathos rather than an old one. Yet there
is one circumstance which does render important the
fact that *A Tale of Two Cities* is one of the later works
of Dickens. This fact is the fact of his dependence
upon another of the great writers of the Victorian era.
And it is in connection with this that we can best see
the truth of which I have been speaking; the truth that
his actual ignorance of France went with amazing
intuitive perception of the truth about it. It is here
that he has most clearly the plain mark of the man
of genius; that he can understand what he does not
understand.

Dickens was inspired to the study of the French
Revolution and to the writing of a romance about it
by the example and influence of Carlyle. Thomas
Carlyle undoubtedly rediscovered for Englishmen the
revolution that was at the back of all their policies
and reforms. It is an entertaining side joke that the
French Revolution should have been discovered for
Britons by the only British writer who did not really
believe in it. Nevertheless, the most authoritative
and the most recent critics on that great renaissance
agree in considering Carlyle's work one of the most
searching and detailed power. Carlyle had read a great
deal about the French Revolution. Dickens had read
nothing at all, except Carlyle. Carlyle was a man who
collected his ideas by the careful collation of documents
and the verification of references. Dickens was a
man who collected his ideas from loose hints in the
streets, and those always the same streets; as I have
said, he was the citizen of one city. Carlyle was in his

way learned; Dickens was in every way ignorant.
Dickens was an Englishman cut off from France;
Carlyle was a Scotsman, historically connected with
France.   And yet, when all this is said and certified,
Dickens is more right than Carlyle.   Dickens's French
Revolution is probably more like the real French
Revolution than Carlyle's.   It is difficult, if not impossible, to state the grounds of this strong conviction.
One can only talk of it by employing that excellent
method which Cardinal Newman employed when
he spoke of the "notes" of Catholicism.   There were
certain "notes" of the Revolution.   One note of the
Revolution was the thing which silly people call optimism, and sensible people call high spirits.   Carlyle
could never quite get it, because with all his spiritual
energy he had no high spirits.   That is why he preferred
prose to poetry.   He could understand rhetoric; for
rhetoric means singing with an object.   But he could
not understand lyrics; for the lyric means singing without an object; as every one does when he is happy.
Now for all its blood and its black guillotines, the French
Revolution was full of mere high spirits.   Nay, it was
full of happiness.   This actual lilt and levity Carlyle
never really found in the Revolution, because he could
not find it in himself.   Dickens knew less of the Revolution, but he had more of it.   When Dickens attacked
abuses, he battered them down with exactly that sort of
cheery and quite one-sided satisfaction with which the
French mob battered down the Bastille.   Dickens
utterly and innocently believed in certain things;
he would, I think, have drawn the sword for them.
Carlyle half believed in half a hundred things; he was at

once more of a mystic and more of a sceptic. Carlyle was the perfect type of the grumbling servant; the old grumbling servant of the aristocratic comedies. He followed the aristocracy, but he growled as he followed. He was obedient without being servile, just as Caleb Balderstone was obedient without being servile. But Dickens was the type of the man who might really have rebelled instead of grumbling. He might have gone out into the street and fought, like the man who took the Bastille. It is somewhat nationally significant that when we talk of the man in the street it means a figure silent, slouching, and even feeble. When the French speak of the man in the street, it means danger in the street.

No one can fail to notice this deep difference between Dickens and the Carlyle whom he avowedly copied. Splendid and symbolic as are Carlyle's scenes of the French Revolution, we have in reading them a curious sense that everything is happening at night. In Dickens even massacre happens by daylight. Carlyle always assumes that because things were tragedies therefore the men who did them felt tragic. Dickens knows that the man who works the worst tragedies is the man who feels comic; as for example, Mr. Quilp. The French Revolution was a much simpler world than Carlyle could understand; for Carlyle was subtle and not simple. Dickens could understand it, for he was simple and not subtle. He understood that plain rage against plain political injustice; he understood again that obvious vindictiveness and that obvious brutality which followed. "Cruelty and the abuse of absolute power," he told an American slave-owner, "are two of

the bad passions of human nature." Carlyle was
quite incapable of rising to the height of that uplifted
common-sense. He must always find something
mystical about the cruelty of the French Revolution.
The effect was equally bad whether he found it mystically bad and called the thing anarchy, or whether he
found it mystically good and called it the rule of the
strong. In both cases he could not understand the
common-sense justice or the common-sense vengeance
of Dickens and the French Revolution.

Yet Dickens has in this book given a perfect and final
touch to this whole conception of mere rebellion and
mere human nature. Carlyle had written the story
of the French Revolution and had made the story a
mere tragedy. Dickens writes the story about the
French Revolution, and does not make the Revolution
itself the tragedy at all. Dickens knows that an out-
break is seldom a tragedy; generally it is the avoidance
of a tragedy. All the real tragedies are silent. Men
fight each other with furious cries, because men fight
each other with chivalry and an unchangeable sense of
brotherhood. But trees fight each other in utter still-
ness; because they fight each other cruelly and without
quarter. In this book, as in history, the guillotine is
not the calamity, but rather the solution of the calamity.
The sin of Sydney Carton is a sin of habit, not of revolution. His gloom is the gloom of London, not the gloom
of Paris.

GREAT EXPECTATIONS

Great Expectations, which was written in the afternoon of Dickens's life and fame, has a quality of serene irony and even sadness, which puts it quite alone among his other works. At no time could Dickens possibly be called cynical, he had too much vitality; but relatively to the other books this book is cynical; but it has the soft and gentle cynicism of old age, not the hard cynicism of youth. To be a young cynic is to be a young brute; but Dickens, who had been so perfectly romantic and sentimental in his youth, could afford to admit this touch of doubt into the mixed experience of his middle age. At no time could any books by Dickens have been called Thackerayan. Both of the two men were too great for that. But relatively to the other Dickensian productions this book may be called Thackerayan. It is a study in human weakness and the slow human surrender. It describes how easily a free lad of fresh and decent instincts can be made to care more for rank and pride and the degrees of our stratified society than for old affection and for honour. It is an extra chapter to *The Book of Snobs*.

The best way of stating the change which this book marks in Dickens can be put in one phrase. In this book for the first time the hero disappears. The hero had descended to Dickens by a long line which

begins with the gods, nay, perhaps if one may say so,
which begins with God. First comes Deity and then
the image of Deity; first comes the god and then the
demi-god, the Hercules who labours and conquers
before he receives his heavenly crown. That idea, with
continual mystery and modification, has continued behind all romantic tales; the demi-god became the hero
of paganism; the hero of paganism became the knight-
errant of Christianity; the knight-errant who wandered
and was foiled before he triumphed became the hero of
the later prose romance, the romance in which the hero
had to fight a duel with the villain but always survived,
in which the hero drove desperate horses through the
night in order to rescue the heroine, but always rescued
her.

This heroic modern hero, this demi-god in a top-hat,
may be said to reach his supreme moment and typical
example about the time when Dickens was writing that
thundering and thrilling and highly unlikely scene in
Nicholas Nickleby, the scene where Nicholas hopelessly
denounces the atrocious Gride in his hour of grinning
triumph, and a thud upon the floor above tells them
that the heroine's tyrannical father has died just in
time to set her free. That is the apotheosis of the pure
heroic as Dickens found it, and as Dickens in some
sense continued it. It may be that it does not appear
with quite so much unmistakable youth, beauty,
valour, and virtue as it does in Nicholas Nickleby.
Walter Gay is a simpler and more careless hero, but
when he is doing any of the business of the story he is
purely heroic. Kit Nubbles is a humbler hero, but he
is a hero; when he is good he is very good. Even

David Copperfield, who confesses to boyish tremors and boyish evasions in his account of his boyhood, acts the strict stiff part of the chivalrous gentleman in all the active and determining scenes of the tale. But *Great Expectations* may be called, like *Vanity Fair*, a novel without a hero. Almost all Thackeray's novels except *Esmond* are novels without a hero, but only one of Dickens's novels can be so described. I do not mean that it is a novel without a *jeune premier*, a young man to make love; *Pickwick* is that and *Oliver Twist*, and, perhaps, *The Old Curiosity Shop*. I mean that it is a novel without a hero in the same far deeper and more deadly sense in which *Pendennis* is also a novel without a hero. I mean that it is a novel which aims chiefly at showing that the hero is unheroic.

All such phrases as these must appear of course to overstate the case. Pip is a much more delightful person than Nicholas Nickleby. Or to take a stronger case for the purpose of our argument, Pip is a much more delightful person than Sydney Carton. Still the fact remains. Most of Nicholas Nickleby's personal actions are meant to show that he is heroic. Most of Pip's actions are meant to show that he is not heroic. The study of Sydney Carton is meant to indicate that with all his vices Sydney Carton was a hero. The study of Pip is meant to indicate that with all his virtues Pip was a snob. The motive of the literary explanation is different. Pip and Pendennis are meant to show how circumstances can corrupt men. Sam Weller and Hercules are meant to show how heroes can subdue circumstances.

This is the preliminary view of the book which is

necessary if we are to regard it as a real and separate
fact in the life of Dickens. Dickens had many moods
because he was an artist; but he had one great mood,
because he was a great artist. Any real difference
therefore from the general drift, or rather (I apologise
to Dickens) the general drive of his creation is very important. This is the one place in his work in which he
does, I will not say feel like Thackeray, far less think
like Thackeray, less still write like Thackeray, but
this is the one of his works in which he understands
Thackeray. He puts himself in some sense in the same
place; he considers mankind at somewhat the same
angle as mankind is considered in one of the sociable
and sarcastic novels of Thackeray. When he deals
with Pip he sets out not to show his strength like the
strength of Hercules, but to show his weakness like the
weakness of Pendennis. When he sets out to describe
Pip's great expectation he does not set out, as in a fairy
tale, with the idea that these great expectations will be
fulfilled; he sets out from the first with the idea that
these great expectations will be disappointing. We
might very well, as I have remarked elsewhere, apply
to all Dickens's books the title *Great Expectations*. All
his books are full of an airy and yet ardent expectation
of everything; of the next person who shall happen to
speak, of the next chimney that shall happen to smoke,
of the next event, of the next ecstasy; of the next
fulfilment of any eager human fancy. All his books
might be called *Great Expectations*. But the only book
to which he gave the name of *Great Expectations* was
the only book in which the expectation was never
realised. It was so with the whole of that splendid and

unconscious generation to which he belonged. The whole glory of that old English middle class was that it was unconscious; its excellence was entirely in that, that it was the culture of the nation, and that it did not know it. If Dickens had ever known that he was optimistic, he would have ceased to be happy.

It is necessary to make this first point clear: that in *Great Expectations* Dickens was really trying to be a quiet, a detached, and even a cynical observer of human life. Dickens was trying to be Thackeray. And the final and startling triumph of Dickens is this: that even to this moderate and modern story, he gives an incomparable energy which is not moderate and which is not modern. He is trying to be reasonable; but in spite of himself he is inspired. He is trying to be detailed, but in spite of himself he is gigantic. Compared to the rest of Dickens this is Thackeray; but compared to the whole of Thackeray we can only say in supreme praise of it that it is Dickens.

Take, for example, the one question of snobbishness. Dickens has achieved admirably the description of the doubts and vanities of the wretched Pip as he walks down the street in his new gentlemanly clothes, the clothes of which he is so proud and so ashamed. Nothing could be so exquisitely human, nothing especially could be so exquisitely masculine as that combination of self-love and self-assertion and even insolence with a naked and helpless sensibility to the slightest breath of ridicule. Pip thinks himself better than every one else, and yet anybody can snub him; that is the everlasting male, and perhaps the everlasting gentleman. Dickens has described perfectly this quivering and defenceless dignity. Dickens has described perfectly how ill-armed it is against the coarse humour of real humanity—the real humanity which Dickens loved, but which idealists and philanthropists do not love, the humanity of cabmen and costermongers and men singing in a third-class carriage; the humanity of Trabb's boy. In describing Pip's weakness Dickens is as true and as delicate as Thackeray. But Thackeray might have been easily as true and as delicate as Dickens. This quick and quiet eye for the tremors of mankind is a thing which Dickens possessed, but which others possessed also. George Eliot or Thackeray could have described the weakness of Pip. Exactly what George Eliot and Thackeray could not have described was the vigour of Trabb's boy. There would have been admirable humour and observation in their accounts of that intolerable urchin. Thackeray would have given us little light touches of Trabb's boy, absolutely true to the quality and colour of the humour, just as in his novels of the eighteenth century, the glimpses of Steele or Bolingbroke or Doctor Johnson are exactly and perfectly true to the colour and quality of their humour. George Eliot in her earlier books would have given us shrewd authentic scraps of the real dialect of Trabb's boy, just as she gave us shrewd and authentic scraps of the real talk in a Midland country town. In her later books she would have given us highly rationalistic explanations of Trabb's boy; which we should not have read. But exactly what they could never have given, and exactly what Dickens does give, is the *bounce* of Trabb's boy. It is the real unconquerable rush and energy in a character which was the supreme and quite

indescribable greatness of Dickens. He conquered
by rushes; he attacked in masses; he carried things
at the spear point in a charge of spears; he was the
Rupert of Fiction. The thing about any figure of
Dickens, about Sam Weller or Dick Swiveller, or
Micawber, or Bagstock, or Trabb's boy,—the thing
about each one of these persons is that he cannot be
exhausted. A Dickens character hits you first on the
nose and then in the waistcoat, and then in the eye and
then in the waistcoat again, with the blinding rapidity
of some battering engine. The scene in which Trabb's
boy continually overtakes Pip in order to reel and stagger as at a first encounter is a thing quite within
the real competence of such a character; it might have
been suggested by Thackeray, or George Eliot, or any
realist. But the point with Dickens is that there is a
rush in the boy's rushings; the writer and the reader
rush with him. They start with him, they stare with
him, they stagger with him, they share an inexpressible
vitality in the air which emanates from this violent and
capering satirist. Trabb's boy is among other things a
boy; he has a physical rapture in hurling himself like a
boomerang and in bouncing to the sky like a ball. It
is just exactly in describing this quality that Dickens is
Dickens and that no one else comes near him. No one
feels in his bones that Felix Holt was strong as he feels in
his bones that little Quilp was strong. No one can feel
that even Rawdon Crawley's splendid smack across the
face of Lord Steyne is quite so living and life-giving as
the "kick after kick" which old Mr. Weller dealt the
dancing and quivering Stiggins as he drove him towards
the trough. This quality, whether expressed intellec-

tually or physically, is the profoundly popular and eternal quality in Dickens; it is the thing that no one else could do. This quality is the quality which has always given its continuous power and poetry to the common people everywhere. It is life; it is the joy of life felt by those who have nothing else but life. It is the thing that all aristocrats have always hated and dreaded in the people. And it is the thing which poor Pip really hates and dreads in Trabb's boy.

A great man of letters or any great artist is symbolic without knowing it. The things he describes are types because they are truths. Shakespeare may, or may not, have ever put it to himself that Richard the Second was a philosophical symbol; but all good criticism must necessarily see him so. It may be a reasonable. question whether the artist should be allegorical. There can be no doubt among sane men that the critic should be allegorical. Spenser may have lost by being less realistic than Fielding. But any good criticism of *Tom Jones* must be as mystical as the *Faery Queen*. Hence it is unavoidable in speaking of a fine book like *Great Expectations* that we should give even to its unpretentious and realistic figures a certain massive mysticism. Pip is Pip, but he is also the well-meaning snob. And this is even more true of those two great figures in the tale which stand for the English democracy. For, indeed, the first and last word upon the English democracy is said in Joe Gargery and Trabb's boy. The actual English populace, as distinct from the French populace or the Scotch or Irish populace, may be said to lie between those two types. The first is the poor man who does not assert himself at all, and the second is the poor man who asserts himself entirely with the weapon of sarcasm. The only way in which the English now ever rise in revolution is under the symbol and leadership of Trabb's boy. What pikes and shillelahs were to the Irish populace, what guns and barricades were to the French populace, that chaff is to the English populace. It is their weapon, the use of which they really understand. It is the one way in which they can make a rich man feel uncomfortable, and they use it very justifiably for all it is worth. If they do not cut off the heads of tyrants at least they sometimes do their best to make the tyrants lose their heads. The gutter boys of the great towns carry the art of personal criticism to so rich and delicate a degree that some well-dressed persons when they walk past a file of them feel as if they were walking past a row of omniscient critics or judges with a power of life and death. Here and there only is some ordinary human custom, some natural human pleasure suppressed in deference to the fastidiousness of the rich. But all the rich tremble before the fastidiousness of the poor.

Of the other type of democracy it is far more difficult to speak. It is always hard to speak of good things or good people, for in satisfying the soul they take away a certain spur to speech. Dickens was often called a sentimentalist. In one sense he sometimes was a sentimentalist. But if sentimentalism be held to mean something artificial or theatrical, then in the core and reality of his character Dickens was the very reverse of a sentimentalist. He seriously and definitely loved goodness. To see sincerity and charity satisfied

him like a meal. What some critics call his love of
sweet stuff is really his love of plain beef and bread.
Sometimes one is tempted to wish that in the long
Dickens dinner the sweet courses could be left out;
but this does not make the whole banquet other than
a banquet singularly solid and simple. The critics
complain of the sweet things, but not because they are
so strong as to like simple things. They complain of
the sweet things because they are so sophisticated as
to like sour things; their tongues are tainted with the
bitterness of absinthe. Yet because of the very simplicity of Dickens's moral tastes it is impossible to
speak adequately of them; and Joe Gargery must
stand as he stands in the book, a thing too obvious to
be understood. But this may be said of him in one
of his minor aspects, that he stands for a certain long-
suffering in the English poor, a certain weary patience
and politeness which almost breaks the heart. One
cannot help wondering whether that great mass of
silent virtue will ever achieve anything on this earth.

OUR MUTUAL FRIEND

Our Mutual Friend marks a happy return to the earlier manner of Dickens at the end of Dickens's life. One might call it a sort of Indian summer of his farce. Those who most truly love Dickens love the earlier Dickens; and any return to his farce must be welcomed, like a young man come back from the dead. In this book indeed he does not merely return to his farce; he returns in a manner to his vulgarity. It is the old democratic and even uneducated Dickens who is writing here. The very title is illiterate. Any priggish pupil teacher could tell Dickens that there is no such phrase in English as "our mutual friend." Any one could tell Dickens that "our mutual friend" means "our reciprocal friend," and that "our reciprocal friend" means nothing. If he had only had all the solemn advantages of academic learning (the absence of which in him was lamented by the *Quarterly Review*), he would have known better. He would have known that the correct phrase for a man known to two people is "our common friend." But if one calls one's friend a common friend, even that phrase is open to misunderstanding.

I dwell with a gloomy pleasure on this mistake in the very title of the book because I, for one, am not pleased to see Dickens gradually absorbed by modern culture and good manners. Dickens, by class and genius, belonged to the kind of people who do talk about a "mutual friend"; and for that class there is a very great deal to be said. These two things can at least be said—that this class does understand the meaning of the word "friend" and the meaning of the word "mutual." I know that for some long time before he had been slowly and subtly sucked into the whirlpool of the fashionable views of later England. I know that in *Bleak House* he treats the aristocracy far more tenderly than he treats them in *David Copperfield*. I know that in *A Tale of Two Cities*, having come under the influence of Carlyle, he treats revolution as strange and weird, whereas under the influence of Cobbett he would have treated it as obvious and reasonable. I know that in *The Mystery of Edwin Drood* he not only praised the Minor Canon of Cloisterham at the expense of the dissenting demagogue, Honeythunder; I know that he even took the last and most disastrous step in the modern English reaction. While blaming the old Cloisterham monks (who were democratic), he praised the old-world peace that they had left behind them—an old-world peace which is simply one of the last amusements of aristocracy. The modern rich feel quite at home with the dead monks. They would have felt anything but comfortable with the live ones. I know, in short, how the simple democracy of Dickens was gradually dimmed by the decay and reaction of the middle of the nineteenth century. I know that he fell into some of the bad habits of aristocratic sentimentalism. I know that he used the word "gentleman" as meaning good man. But all this only adds to the unholy joy with which I realise that the very title of one of his best books was a vulgarism. It is pleasant to contemplate this last unconscious knock in the eye for the gentility with which Dickens was half impressed. Dickens is the old self-made man; you may take him or leave him. He has its disadvantages and its merits. No university man would have written the title; no university man could have written the book.

If it were a mere matter of the accident of a name it would not be worth while thus to dwell on it, even as a preface. But the title is in this respect typical of the tale. The novel called *Our Mutual Friend* is in many ways a real reaction towards the earlier Dickens manner. I have remarked that *Little Dorrit* was a reversion to the form of the first books, but not to their spirit; *Our Mutual Friend* is a reversion to the spirit as well as the form. Compare, for instance, the public figures that make a background in each book. Mr. Merdle is a commercial man having no great connection with the plot; similarly Mr. Podsnap is a commercial man having no great connection with the plot. This is altogether in the spirit of the earlier books; the whole point of an early Dickens novel was to have as many people as possible entirely unconnected with the plot. But exactly because both studies are irrelevant, the contrast between them can be more clearly perceived. Dickens goes out of his way to describe Merdle; and it is a gloomy description. But Dickens goes out of his way to describe Podsnap, and it is a happy and hilarious description. It recalls the days when he hunted great game; when he went out of his way to entrap such adorable monsters as Mr. Pecksniff or Mr. Vincent Crummles. With these wild beings we never bother about the cause of their coming. Such guests in a

14

story may be uninvited, but they are never *de trop*. They earn their night's lodging in any tale by being so uproariously amusing; like little Tommy Tucker in the legend, they sing for their supper. This is really the marked truth about *Our Mutual Friend*, as a stage in the singular latter career of Dickens. It is like the leaping up and flaming of a slowly dying fire. The best things in the book are in the old best manner of the author. They have that great Dickens quality of being something which is pure farce and yet which is not superficial; an unfathomable farce—a farce that goes down to the roots of the universe. The highest compliment that can ever be paid to the humour of Dickens is paid when some lady says, with the sudden sincerity of her sex, that it is "too silly." The phrase is really a perfectly sound and acute criticism. Humour does consist in being too silly, in passing the borderland, in breaking through the floor of sense and falling into some starry abyss of nonsense far below our ordinary human life. This "too silly" quality is really present in *Our Mutual Friend*. It is present in *Our Mutual Friend* just as it is present in *Pickwick*, or *Martin Chuzzlewit;* just as it is not present in *Little Dorrit* or in *Hard Times*. Many tests might be employed. One is the pleasure in purely physical jokes—jokes about the body. The general dislike which every one felt for Mr. Stiggins's nose is of the same kind as the ardent desire which Mr. Lammle felt for Mr. Fledgeby's nose. "Give me your nose, Sir," said Mr. Lammle. That sentence alone would be enough to show that the young Dickens had never died.

The opening of a book goes for a great deal. The

opening of *Our Mutual Friend* is much more instinctively energetic and light-hearted than that of any of the other novels of his concluding period. Dickens had always enough optimism to make his stories end well. He had not, in his later years, always enough optimism to make them begin well. Even *Great Expectations*, the saddest of his later books, ends well; it ends well in spite of himself, who had intended it to end badly. But if we leave the evident case of good endings and take the case of good beginnings, we see how much *Our Mutual Friend* stands out from among the other novels of the evening or the end of Dickens. The tale of *Little Dorrit* begins in a prison. One of the prisoners is a villain, and his villainy is as dreary as the prison; that might matter nothing. But the other prisoner is vivacious, and even his vivacity is dreary. The first note struck is sad. In the tale of *Edwin Drood* the first scene is in an opium den, suffocated with every sort of phantasy and falsehood. Nor is it true that these openings are merely accidental; they really cast their shadow over the tales. The people of *Little Dorrit* begin in prison; and it is the whole point of the book that people never get out of prison. The story of *Edwin Drood* begins amid the fumes of opium, and it never gets out of the fumes of opium. The darkness of that strange and horrible smoke is deliberately rolled over the whole story. Dickens, in his later years, permitted more and more his story to take the cue from its inception. All the more remarkable, therefore, is the real jerk and spurt of good spirits with which he opens *Our Mutual Friend*. It begins with a good piece of rowdy satire, wildly exaggerated and extremely true.

It belongs to the same class as the first chapter of *Martin Chuzzlewit*, with its preposterous pedigree of the Chuzzlewit family, or even the first chapter of *Pickwick*, with its immortal imbecilities about the Theory of Tittlebats and Mr. Blotton of Aldgate.   Doubtless the early satiric chapter in *Our Mutual Friend* is of a more strategic and ingenious kind of satire than can be found in these early and explosive parodies.   Still, there is a quality common to both, and that quality is the whole of Dickens.   It is a quality difficult to define—hence the whole difficulty of criticising Dickens.   Perhaps it can be best stated in two separate statements or as two separate symptoms.   The first is the mere fact that the reader rushes to read it.   The second is the mere fact that the writer rushed to write it.

This beginning, which is like a burst of the old exuberant Dickens, is, of course, the Veneering dinner-party.   In its own way it is as good as anything that Dickens ever did.   There is the old faculty of managing a crowd, of making character clash with character, that had made Dickens not only the democrat but even the demagogue of fiction.   For if it is hard to manage a mob, it is hardest of all to manage a swell mob.   The particular kind of chaos that is created by the hospitality of a rich upstart has perhaps never been so accurately and outrageously described.   Every touch about the thing is true; to this day any one can test it if he goes to a dinner of this particular kind.   How admirable, for instance, is the description of the way in which all the guests ignored the host; how the host and hostess peered and gaped for some stray attention as if they had been a pair of poor relations.   Again, how well, as a matter

of social colour, the distinctions between the type and
tone of the guests are made even in the matter of this
unguestlike insolence. How well Dickens distinguishes
the ill-bred indifference of Podsnap from the well-bred
indifference of Mortimer Lightwood and Eugene Wray-
burn. How well he distinguishes the bad manners of
the merchant from the equally typical bad manners of
the gentleman. Above all, how well he catches the
character of the creature who is really the master of all
these: the impenetrable male servant. Nowhere in
literature is the truth about servants better told.
For that truth is simply this: that the secret of aristocracy is hidden even from aristocrats. Servants, butlers,
footmen, are the high priests who have the real dis-
pensation; and even gentlemen are afraid of them.
Dickens was never more right than when he made the
new people, the Veneerings, employ a butler who despised
not only them but all their guests and acquaintances.
The admirable person called the Analytical Chemist
shows his perfection particularly in the fact that he regards all the sham gentlemen and all the real gentlemen
with the same gloomy and incurable contempt. He
offers wine to the offensive Podsnap or the shrieking
Tippins with a melancholy sincerity and silence; but
he offers his letter to the aristocratic and unconscious
Mortimer with the same sincerity and with the same
silence. It is a great pity that the Analytical Chemist
only occurs in two or three scenes of this excellent story.
As far as I know, he never really says a word from one
end of the book to the other; but he is one of the best
characters in Dickens.

Round the Veneering dinner-table are collected not

indeed the best characters in Dickens, but certainly
the best characters in *Our Mutual Friend*. Certainly
one exception must be made. Fledgeby is unaccount-
ably absent. There was really no reason why he should
not have been present at a dinner-party given by the
Veneerings and including the Lammles. His money
was at least more genuine than theirs. If he had been
present the party would really have included all that
is important in *Our Mutual Friend*. For indeed, outside Mr. Fledgeby and the people at the dinner-party,
there is something a little heavy and careless about the
story. Mr. Silas Wegg is really funny; and he serves
the purpose of a necessary villain in the plot. But his
humour and his villainy seem to have no particular connection with each other; when he is not scheming he
seems the last man likely to scheme. He is rather like
one of Dickens's agreeable Bohemians, a pleasant com-
panion, a quoter of fine verses. His villainy seems an
artificial thing attached to him, like his wooden leg.
For while his villainy is supposed to be of a dull, mean,
and bitter sort (quite unlike, for instance, the uproarious
villainy of Quilp), his humour is of the sincere, flowing
and lyric character, like that of Dick Swiveller or Mr.
Micawber. He tells Mr. Boffin that he will drop into
poetry in a friendly way. He does drop into it in a
friendly way; in much too really a friendly way to make
him convincing as a mere calculating knave. He and
Mr. Venus are such natural and genuine companions
that one does not see why if Venus repents Wegg should
not repent too. In short, Wegg is a convenience for a
plot and not a very good plot at that. But if he is
one of the blots on the business, he is not the principal

one. If the real degradation of Wegg is not very convincing, it is at least immeasurably more convincing than the pretended degradation of Boffin. The passage in which Boffin appears as a sort of miser, and then afterwards explains that he only assumed the character for reasons of his own, has something about it highly jerky and unsatisfactory. The truth of the whole matter I think, almost certainly, is that Dickens did not originally mean Boffin's lapse to be fictitious. He originally meant Boffin really to be corrupted by wealth, slowly to degenerate and as slowly to repent. But the story went too quickly for this long, double, and difficult process; therefore Dickens at the last moment made a sudden recovery possible by representing that the whole business had been a trick. Consequently, this episode is not an error merely in the sense that we may find many errors in a great writer like Dickens; it is a mistake patched up with another mistake. It is a case of that ossification which occurs round the healing of an actual fracture; the story had broken down and been mended.

If Dickens had fulfilled what was probably his original design, and described the slow freezing of Boffin's soul in prosperity, I do not say that he would have done the thing well. He was not good at describing change in anybody, especially not good at describing a change for the worse. The tendency of all his characters is upwards, like bubbles, never downwards, like stones. But at least it would probably have been more credible than the story as it stands; for the story as it stands is actually less credible than any conceivable kind of moral ruin for Boffin. Such a character as his—rough, simple and lumberingly unconscious—might be more easily conceived as really sinking in self-respect and honour than as keeping up, month after month, so strained and inhuman a theatrical performance. To a good man (of that particular type) it would be easier to be bad than to pretend to be bad. It might have taken years to turn Noddy Boffin into a miser; but it would have taken centuries to turn him into an actor. This unreality in the later Boffin scenes makes the end of the story of John Harmon somewhat more unimpressive perhaps than it might otherwise have been. Upon no hypothesis, however, can he be made one of the more impressive figures of Dickens. It is true that it is an unfair criticism to object, as some have done, that Dickens does not succeed in disguising the identity of John Harmon with John Rokesmith. Dickens never intended to disguise it; the whole story would be mainly unintelligible and largely uninteresting if it had been successfully disguised. But though John Harmon or Rokesmith was never intended to be merely a man of mystery, it is not quite so easy to say what he was intended to be. Bella is a possible and pretty sketch. Mrs. Wilfer, her mother, is an entirely impossible and entirely delightful one. Miss Podsnap is not only excellent, she is to a healthy taste positively attractive; there is a real suggestion in her of the fact that humility is akin to truth, even when humility takes its more comic form of shyness. There is not in all literature a more human *cri de cœur* than that with which Georgiana Podsnap receives the information that a young man has professed himself to be attracted by her—"Oh what a Fool he must be!"

Two other figures require praise, though they are in

the more tragic manner which Dickens touched from time to time in his later period. Bradley Headstone is really a successful villain; so successful that he fully captures our sympathies. Also there is something original in the very conception. It was a new notion to add to the villains of fiction, whose thoughts go quickly, this villain whose thoughts go slow but sure; and it was a new notion to combine a deadly criminality not with high life or the slums (the usual haunts for villains) but with the laborious respectability of the lower, middle classes. The other good conception is the boy, Bradley Headstone's pupil, with his dull, inexhaustible egoism, his pert, unconscious cruelty, and the strict decorum and incredible baseness of his views of life. It is singular that Dickens, who was not only a radical and a social reformer, but one who would have been particularly concerned to maintain the principle of modern popular education, should nevertheless have seen so clearly this potential evil in the mere educationalism of our time—the fact that merely educating the democracy may easily mean setting to work to despoil it of all the democratic virtues. It is better to be Lizzie Hexam and not know how to read and write than to be Charlie Hexam and not know how to appreciate Lizzie Hexam. It is not only necessary that the democracy should be taught; it is also necessary that the democracy should be taught democracy. Otherwise it will certainly fall a victim to that snobbishness and system of worldly standards which is the most natural and easy of all the forms of human corruption. This is one of the many dangers which Dickens saw before it existed. Dickens was really a prophet; far more of a prophet than Carlyle.

EDWIN DROOD

Pickwick was a work partly designed by others, but ultimately filled up by Dickens. *Edwin Drood*, the last book, was a book designed by Dickens, but ultimately filled up by others. The *Pickwick Papers* showed how much Dickens could make out of other people's suggestions; *The Mystery of Edwin Drood* shows how very little other people can make out of Dickens's suggestions.

Dickens was meant by Heaven to be the great melodramatist; so that even his literary end was melodramatic. Something more seems hinted at in the cutting short of *Edwin Drood* by Dickens than the mere cutting short of a good novel by a great man. It seems rather like the last taunt of some elf, leaving the world, that it should be this story which is not ended, this story which is only a story. The only one of Dickens's novels which he did not finish was the only one that really needed finishing. He never had but one thoroughly good plot to tell; and that he has only told in heaven. This is what separates the case in question from any parallel cases of novelists cut off in the act of creation. That great novelist, for instance, with whom Dickens is constantly compared, died also in the middle of *Denis Duval*. But any one can see in *Denis Duval* the qualities of the later work of Thackeray; the

increasing discursiveness, the increasing retrospective
poetry, which had been in part the charm and in part
the failure of *Philip* and *The Virginians*. But to
Dickens it was permitted to die at a dramatic moment
and to leave a dramatic mystery. Any Thackerayan
could have completed the plot of *Denis Duval*; except
indeed that a really sympathetic Thackerayan might
have had some doubt as to whether there was any plot
to complete. But Dickens, having had far too little
plot in his stories previously, had far too much plot
in the story he never told. Dickens dies in the act of
telling, not his tenth novel, but his first news of murder.
He drops down dead as he is in the act of denouncing
the assassin. It is permitted to Dickens, in short, to
come to a literary end as strange as his literary beginning. He began by completing the old romance of
travel. He ended by inventing the new detective story.

It is as a detective story first and last that we have
to consider *The Mystery of Edwin Drood*. This does not
mean, of course, that the details are not often admirable
in their swift and penetrating humour; to say that of
the book would be to say that Dickens did not write it.
Nothing could be truer, for instance, than the manner
in which the dazed and drunken dignity of Durdles
illustrates a certain bitterness at the bottom of the
bewilderment of the poor. Nothing could be better
than the way in which the haughty and allusive conversation between Miss Twinkleton and the landlady
illustrates the maddening preference of some females
for skating upon thin social ice. There is an even
better example than these of the original humorous
insight of Dickens; and one not very often remarked,

because of its brevity and its unimportance in the narrative. But Dickens never did anything better than the short account of Mr. Grewgious's dinner being brought from the tavern by two waiters: "a stationary waiter," and "a flying waiter." The "flying waiter" brought the food and the "stationary waiter" quarrelled with him; the "flying waiter" brought glasses and the "stationary waiter" looked through them. Finally, it will be remembered the "stationary waiter" left the room, casting a glance which indicated "let it be understood that all emoluments are mine, and that Nil is the reward of this slave." Still, Dickens wrote the book as a detective story; he wrote it as *The Mystery of Edwin Drood*. And alone, perhaps, among detective-story writers, he never lived to destroy his mystery. Here alone then among the Dickens novels it is necessary to speak of the plot and of the plot alone. And when we speak of the plot it becomes immediately necessary to speak of the two or three standing explanations which celebrated critics have given of the plot.

The story, so far as it was written by Dickens, can be read here. It describes, as will be seen, the disappearance of the young architect Edwin Drood after a night of festivity which was supposed to celebrate his reconciliation with a temporary enemy, Neville Landless, and was held at the house of his uncle John Jasper. Dickens continued the tale long enough to explain or explode the first and most obvious of his riddles. Long before the existing part terminates it has become evident that Drood has been put away, not by his obvious opponent, Landless, but by his uncle who professes for him an almost painful affection. The fact

that we all know this, however, ought not in fairness to
blind us to the fact that, considered as the first fraud in
a detective story, it has been, with great skill, at once
suggested and concealed. Nothing, for instance,
could be cleverer as a piece of artistic mystery than the
fact that Jasper, the uncle, always kept his eyes fixed
on Drood's face with a dark and watchful tenderness;
the thing is so told that at first we really take it as only
indicating something morbid in the affection; it is only
afterwards that the frightful fancy breaks upon us that
it is not morbid affection but morbid antagonism. This
first mystery (which is no longer a mystery) of Jasper's
guilt, is only worth remarking because it shows that
Dickens meant and felt himself able to mask all his
batteries with real artistic strategy and artistic caution.
The manner of the unmasking of Jasper marks the
manner and tone in which the whole tale was to be told.
Here we have not got to do with Dickens simply giving
himself away, as he gave himself away in *Pickwick* or
The Christmas Carol. Not that one complains of his
giving himself away; there was no better gift.

What was the mystery of Edwin Drood from Dickens's point of view we shall never know, except perhaps
from Dickens in heaven, and then he will very likely
have forgotten. But the mystery of Edwin Drood
from our point of view, from that of his critics, and
those who have with some courage (after his death)
attempted to be his collaborators, is simply this.
There is no doubt that Jasper either murdered Drood
or supposed that he had murdered him. This certainty
we have from the fact that it is the whole point of a
scene between Jasper and Drood's lawyer Grewgious

in which Jasper is struck down with remorse when he realises that Drood has been killed (from his point of view) needlessly and without profit. The only question is whether Jasper's remorse was as needless as his murder. In other words the only question is whether, while he certainly thought he had murdered Drood, he had really done it. It need hardly be said that such a doubt would not have been raised for nothing; gentlemen like Jasper do not as a rule waste good remorse except upon successful crime. The origin of the doubt about the real death of Drood is this. Towards the latter end of the existing chapters there appears very abruptly, and with a quite ostentatious air of mystery, a character called Datchery. He appears for the purpose of spying upon Jasper and getting up some case against him; at any rate, if he has not this purpose in the story he has no other earthly purpose in it. He is an old gentleman of juvenile energy, with a habit of carrying his hat in his hand even in the open air; which some have interpreted as meaning that he feels the unaccustomed weight of a wig. Now there are one or two people in the story who this person might possibly be. Notably there is one person in the story who seems as if he were meant to be something, but who hitherto has certainly been nothing; I mean Bazzard, Mr. Grewgious's clerk, a sulky fellow interested in theatricals, of whom an unnecessary fuss is made. There is also Mr. Grewgious himself, and there is also another suggestion, so much more startling that I shall have to deal with it later.

For the moment, however, the point is this: That ingenious writer, Mr. Proctor, started the highly plausible theory that this Datchery was Drood himself, who had not really been killed. He adduced a most complex and complete scheme covering nearly all the details; but the strongest argument he had was rather one of general artistic effect. This argument has been quite perfectly summed up by Mr. Andrew Lang in one sentence: "If Edwin Drood is dead, there is not much mystery about him." This is quite true; Dickens, when writing in so deliberate, nay, dark and conspiratorial a manner, would surely have kept the death of Drood and the guilt of Jasper hidden a little longer if the only real mystery had been the guilt of Jasper and the death of Drood. It certainly seems artistically more likely that there was a further mystery of Edwin Drood; not the mystery that he was murdered, but the mystery that he was not murdered. It is true indeed that Mr. Cumming Walters has a theory of Datchery (to which I have already darkly alluded) a theory which is wild enough to be the centre not only of any novel but of any harlequinade. But the point is that even Mr. Cumming Walters's theory, though it makes the mystery more extraordinary, does not make it any more of a mystery of Edwin Drood. It should not have been called *The Mystery of Drood*, but *The Mystery of Datchery*. This is the strongest case for Proctor; if the story tells of Drood coming back as Datchery, the story does at any rate fulfil the title upon its title-page.

The principal objection to Proctor's theory is that there seems no adequate reason why Jasper should not have murdered his nephew if he wanted to. And there seems even less reason why Drood, if unsuccessfully murdered, should not have raised the alarm. Happy young architects, when nearly strangled by elderly organists, do not generally stroll away and come back some time afterwards in a wig and with a false name. Superficially it would seem almost as odd to find the murderer investigating the origin of the murder, as to find the corpse investigating it. To this problem two of the ablest literary critics of our time, Mr. Andrew Lang and Mr. William Archer (both of them persuaded generally of the Proctor theory) have especially addressed themselves. Both have come to the same substantial conclusion; and I suspect that they are right. They hold that Jasper (whose mania for opium is much insisted on in the tale) had some sort of fit, or trance, or other physical seizure as he was committing the crime so that he left it unfinished; and they also hold that he had drugged Drood, so that Drood, when he recovered from the attack, was doubtful about who had been his assailant. This might really explain, if a little fancifully, his coming back to the town in the character of a detective. He might think it due to his uncle (whom he last remembered in a kind of murderous vision) to make an independent investigation as to whether he was really guilty or not. He might say, as Hamlet said of a vision equally terrifying, "I 'll have grounds more relative than this." In fairness it must be said that there is something vaguely shaky about this theory; chiefly, I think, in this respect; that there is a sort of farcical cheerfulness about Datchery which does not seem altogether appropriate to a lad who ought to be in an agony of doubt as to whether his best friend was or was not his assassin. Still there are many such incon-

gruities in Dickens; and the explanation of Mr. Archer
and Mr. Lang is an explanation. I do not believe that
any explanation as good can be given to account for the
tale being called *The Mystery of Edwin Drood*, if the tale
practically starts with his corpse.

If Drood is really dead one cannot help feeling the
story ought to end where it does end, not by accident
but by design. The murder is explained. Jasper is
ready to be hanged, and every one else in a decent novel
ought to be ready to be married. If there was to be
much more of anything, it must have been of anti-
climax. Nevertheless there are degrees of anti-
climax. Some of the more obvious explanations of
Datchery are quite reasonable, but they are distinctly
tame. For instance, Datchery may be Bazzard; but
it is not very exciting if he is; for we know nothing
about Bazzard and care less. Again, he might be
Grewgious; but there is something pointless about one
grotesque character dressing up as another grotesque
character actually less amusing than himself. Now,
Mr. Cumming Walters has at least had the distinction
of inventing a theory which makes the story at least an
interesting story, even if it is not exactly the story that
is promised on the cover of the book. The obvious
enemy of Drood, on whom suspicion first falls, the
swarthy and sulky Landless, has a sister even swarthier
and, except for her queenly dignity, even sulkier than he.
This barbaric princess is evidently meant to be (in a
sombre way) in love with Crisparkle, the clergyman and
muscular Christian who represents the breezy element
in the emotions of the tale. Mr. Cumming Walters
seriously maintains that it is this barbaric princess

who puts on a wig and dresses up as Mr. Datchery. He
urges his case with much ingenuity of detail. Helena
Landless certainly had a motive; to save her brother,
who was accused falsely, by accusing Jasper justly.
She certainly had some of the faculties; it is elaborately
stated in the earlier part of her story that she was
accustomed as a child to dress up in male costume and
run into the wildest adventures. There may be something in Mr. Cumming Walters's argument that the
very flippancy of Datchery is the self-conscious flippancy of a strong woman in such an odd situation; certainly there is the same flippancy in Portia and in
Rosalind. Nevertheless, I think, there is one final
objection to the theory; and that is simply this, that
it is comic. It is generally wrong to represent a great
master of the grotesque as being grotesque exactly
where he does not intend to be. And I am persuaded
that if Dickens had really meant Helena to turn into
Datchery, he would have made her from the first in some
way more light, eccentric, and laughable; he would
have made her at least as light and laughable as Rosa.
As it is, there is something strangely stiff and incredible
about the idea of a lady so dark and dignified dressing
up as a swaggering old gentleman in a blue coat and
grey trousers. We might almost as easily imagine
Edith Dombey dressing up as Major Bagstock. We
might almost as easily imagine Rebecca in *Ivanhoe*
dressing up as Isaac of York.

Of course such a question can never really be settled
precisely, because it is the question not merely of a
mystery but of a puzzle. For here the detective novel
differs from every other kind of novel. The ordinary

novelist desires to keep his readers to the point; the
detective novelist actually desires to keep his readers
off the point. In the first case, every touch must help
to tell the reader what he means; in the second case,
most of the touches must conceal or even contradict
what he means. You are supposed to see and appreciate the smallest gestures of a good actor; but you do not
see all the gestures of a conjuror, if he is a good conjuror.
Hence, into the critical estimate of such works as this,
there is introduced a problem, an extra perplexity,
which does not exist in other cases. I mean the problem of the things commonly called blinds. Some of
the points which we pick out as suggestive may have
been put in as deceptive. Thus the whole conflict
between a critic with one theory, like Mr. Lang, and a
critic with another theory, like Mr. Cumming Walters,
becomes eternal and a trifle farcical. Mr. Walters says
that all Mr. Lang's clues were blinds; Mr. Lang says
that all Mr. Walters's clues were blinds. Mr. Walters
can say that some passages seemed to show that Helena
was Datchery; Mr. Lang can reply that those passages
were only meant to deceive simple people like Mr.
Walters into supposing that she was Datchery. Similarly Mr. Lang can say that the return of Drood is
foreshadowed; and Mr. Walters can reply that it was
foreshadowed because it was never meant to come off.
There seems no end to this insane process; anything
that Dickens wrote may or may not mean the opposite
of what it says. Upon this principle I should be very
ready for one to declare that all the suggested Datcherys
were really blinds; merely because they can naturally be
suggested. I would undertake to maintain that Mr.

Datchery is really Miss Twinkleton, who has a mercenary interest in keeping Rosa Budd at her school. This suggestion does not seem to me to be really much more humorous than Mr. Cumming Walters's theory. Yet either may certainly be true. Dickens is dead, and a number of splendid scenes and startling adventures have died with him. Even if we get the right solution we shall not know that it is right. The tale might have been, and yet it has not been.

And I think there is no thought so much calculated to make one doubt death itself, to feel that sublime doubt which has created all religion—the doubt that found death incredible. Edwin Drood may or may not have really died; but surely Dickens did not really die. Surely our real detective liveth and shall appear in the latter days of the earth. For a finished tale may give a man immortality in the light and literary sense; but an unfinished tale suggests another immortality, more essential and more strange.

MASTER HUMPHREY'S CLOCK

It is quite indispensable to include a criticism of *Master Humphrey's Clock* in any survey of Dickens, although it is not one of the books of which his admirers would chiefly boast; although perhaps it is almost the only one of which he would not have boasted himself. As a triumph of Dickens, at least, it is not of great importance. But as a sample of Dickens it happens to be of quite remarkable importance. The very fact that it is for the most part somewhat more level and even monotonous than most of his creations, makes us realise, as it were, against what level and monotony those creations commonly stand out. This book is the background of his mind. It is the basis and minimum of him which was always there. Alone, of all written things, this shows how he felt when he was not writing. Dickens might have written it in his sleep. That is to say, it is written by a sluggish Dickens, a half automatic Dickens, a dreaming and drifting Dickens; but still by the enduring Dickens.

But this truth can only be made evident by beginning nearer to the root of the matter. *Nicholas Nickleby* had just completed, or, to speak more strictly, confirmed, the popularity of the young author; wonderful as *Pickwick* was it might have been a nine days' wonder; *Oliver Twist* had been powerful but painful; it was

Nicholas Nickleby that proved the man to be a great
productive force of which one could ask more, of which
one could ask all things. His publishers, Chapman
and Hall, seem to have taken at about this point that
step which sooner or later most publishers do take with
regard to a half successful man who is becoming wholly
successful. Instead of asking him for something,
they asked him for anything. They made him, so to
speak, the editor of his own works. And indeed it is
literally as the editor of his own works that he next
appears; for the next thing to which he proposes to
put his name is not a novel, but for all practical purposes
a magazine. Yet although it is a magazine, it is a
magazine entirely written by himself; the publishers, in
point of fact, wanted to create a kind of Dickens
Miscellany, in a much more literal sense than that in
which we speak of a Bentley Miscellany. Dickens
was in no way disposed to dislike such a job; for the
more miscellaneous he was the more he enjoyed himself.
And indeed this early experiment of his bears a great
deal of resemblance to those later experiences in which
he was the editor of two popular periodicals. The
editor of *Master Humphrey's Clock* was a kind of type
or precursor of the editor of *Household Words* and *All
the Year Round*. There was the same sense of absolute
ease in an atmosphere of infinite gossip. There was
the same great advantage gained by a man of genius
who wrote best scrappily and by episodes. The
omnipotence of the editor helped the eccentricities
of the author. He could excuse himself for all his own
shortcomings. He could begin a novel, get tired of it,
and turn it into a short story. He could begin a short

story, get fond of it, and turn it into a novel. Thus in
the days of *Household Words* he could begin a big
scheme of stories, such as *Somebody's Luggage*, or
Seven Poor Travellers, and after writing a tale or two
toss the rest to his colleagues. Thus, on the other
hand, in the time of *Master Humphrey's Clock*, he
could begin one small adventure of Master Humphrey
and find himself unable to stop it. It is quite clear I
think (though only from moral evidence, which some
call reading between the lines) that he originally meant
to tell many separate tales of Master Humphrey's
wanderings in London, only one of which, and that
a short one, was to have been concerned with a little
girl going home. Fortunately for us that little girl
had a grandfather, and that grandfather had a curiosity
shop and also a nephew, and that nephew had an
entirely irrelevant friend whom men and angels called
Richard Swiveller. Once having come into the society
of Swiveller it is not unnatural that Dickens stayed
there for a whole book. The essential point for us
here, however, is that *Master Humphrey's Clock* was
stopped by the size and energy of the thing that had
come of it. It died in childbirth.

There is, however, another circumstance which,
even in ordinary public opinion, makes this miscellany
important, besides the great novel that came out of it.
I mean that the ordinary reader can remember one
great thing about *Master Humphrey's Clock*, besides
the fact that it was the frame-work of *The Old Curiosity
Shop*. He remembers that Mr. Pickwick and the
Wellers rise again from the dead. Dickens makes
Samuel Pickwick become a member of Master Hum-

phrey's Clock Society; and he institutes a parallel
society in the kitchen under the name of Mr. Weller's
Watch.

Before we consider the question of whether Dickens
was wise when he did this, it is worth remarking how
really odd it is that this is the only place where he did it.
Dickens, one would have thought, was the one man
who might naturally have introduced old characters
into new stories. Dickens, as a matter of fact, was
almost the one man who never did it. It would have
seemed natural in him for a double reason; first, that
his characters were very valuable to him, and second
that they were not very valuable to his particular
stories. They were dear to him, and they are dear to
us; but they really might as well have turned up
(within reason) in one environment as well as in another.
We, I am sure, should be delighted to meet Mr. Mantalini in the story of *Dombey and Son*. And he certainly would not be much missed from the plot of
Nicholas Nickleby. "I am an affectionate father,"
said Dickens, "to all the children of my fancy; but like
many other parents I have in my heart of hearts a
favourite child; and his name is David Copperfield."
Yet although his heart must often have yearned backwards to the children of his fancy whose tale was already told, yet he never touched one of them again
even with the point of his pen. The characters in
David Copperfield, as in all the others, were dead for
him after he had done the book; if he loved them as
children, it was as dead and sanctified children. It is
a curious test of the strength and even reticence that
underlay the seeming exuberance of Dickens, that he

never did yield at all to exactly that indiscretion or act of sentimentalism which would seem most natural to his emotions and his art. Or rather he never did yield to it except here in this one case; the case of *Master Humphrey's Clock*.

And it must be remembered that nearly everybody else did yield to it. Especially did those writers who are commonly counted Dickens's superiors in art and exactitude and closeness to connected reality. Thackeray wallowed in it; Anthony Trollope lived on it. Those modern artists who pride themselves most on the separation and unity of a work of art have indulged in it often; thus, for instance, Stevenson gave a glimpse of Alan Breck in *The Master of Ballantrae*, and meant to give a glimpse of the Master of Ballantrae in another unwritten tale called *The Rising Sun*. The habit of revising old characters is so strong in Thackeray that *Vanity Fair*, *Pendennis*, *The Newcomes*, and *Philip* are in one sense all one novel. Certainly the reader sometimes forgets which one of them he is reading. Afterwards he cannot remember whether the best description of Lord Steyne's red whiskers or Mr. Wagg's rude jokes occurred in *Vanity Fair*, or *Pendennis;* he cannot remember whether his favourite dialogue between Mr. and Mrs. Pendennis occurred in *The Newcomes*, or in *Philip*. Whenever two Thackeray characters in two Thackeray novels could by any possibility have been contemporary, Thackeray delights to connect them. He makes Major Pendennis nod to Dr. Firmin, and Colonel Newcome ask Major Dobbin to dinner. Whenever two characters could not possibly have been contemporary he goes out of his

way to make one the remote ancestor of the other.
Thus he created the great house of Warrington solely
to connect a "blue-bearded" Bohemian journalist
with the blood of Henry Esmond. It is quite impossible to conceive Dickens keeping up this elaborate
connection between all his characters and all his books,
especially across the ages. It would give us a kind of
shock if we learnt from Dickens that Major Bagstock
was the nephew of Mr. Chester. Still less can we
imagine Dickens carrying on an almost systematic
family chronicle as was in some sense done by Trollope.
There must be some reason for such a paradox; for in
itself it is a very curious one. The writers who wrote
carefully were always putting, as it were, after-words
and appendices to their already finished portraits;
the man who did splendid and flamboyant but faulty
portraits never attempted to touch them up. Or
rather (we may say again) he attempted it once, and
then he failed.

The reason lay, I think, in the very genius of
Dickens's creation. The child he bore of his soul
quitted him when his term was passed like a verit-
able child born of the body. It was independent of
him, as a child is of its parents. It had become dead
to him even in becoming alive. When Thackeray
studied Pendennis or Lord Steyne he was studying
something outside himself, and therefore something
that might come nearer and nearer. But when Dickens
brought forth Sam Weller or Pickwick he was creating
something that had once been inside himself and therefore when once created could only go further and further
away. It may seem a strange thing to say of such

laughable characters and of so lively an author, yet I say it quite seriously; I think it possible that there arose between Dickens and his characters that strange and almost supernatural shyness that arises often between parents and children; because they are too close to each other to be open with each other. Too much hot and high emotion had gone to the creation of one of his great figures for it to be possible for him without embarrassment ever to speak with it again. This is the thing which some fools call fickleness; but which is not the death of feeling, but rather its dreadful perpetuation; this shyness is the final seal of strong sentiment; this coldness is an eternal constancy.

This one case where Dickens broke through his rule was not such a success as to tempt him in any case to try the thing again.

There is weakness in the strict sense of the word in this particular reappearance of Samuel Pickwick and Samuel Weller. In the original *Pickwick Papers* Dickens had with quite remarkable delicacy and vividness contrived to suggest a certain fundamental sturdiness and spirit in that corpulent and complacent old gentleman. Mr. Pickwick was a mild man, a respectable man, a placid man; but he was very decidedly a man. He could denounce his enemies and fight for his nightcap. He was fat; but he had a backbone. In *Master Humphrey's Clock* the backbone seems somehow to be broken; his good nature seems limp instead of alert. He gushes out of his good heart; instead of taking a good heart for granted as a part of any decent gentleman's furniture as did the older and stronger Pickwick. The truth is, I think, that Mr. Pickwick in complete repose loses some part of the whole point of his existence. The quality which makes the *Pickwick Papers* one of the greatest of human fairy tales is a quality which all the great fairy tales possess, and which marks them out from most modern writing. A modern novelist generally endeavours to make his story interesting, by making his hero odd. The most typical modern books are those in which the central figure is himself or herself an exception, a cripple, a courtesan, a lunatic, a swindler, or a person of the most perverse temperament. Such stories, for instance, are *Sir Richard Calmady*, *Dodo*, *Quisante*, *La Bête Humaine*, even the *Egoist*. But in a fairy tale the boy sees all the wonders of fairyland because he is an ordinary boy. In the same way Mr. Samuel Pickwick sees an extraordinary England because he is an ordinary old gentleman. He does not see things through the rosy spectacles of the modern optimist or the green-smoked spectacles of the pessimist; he sees it through the crystal glasses of his own innocence. One must see the world clearly even in order to see its wildest poetry. One must see it sanely even in order to see that it is insane.

Mr. Pickwick, then, relieved against a background of heavy kindliness and quiet club life does not seem to be quite the same heroic figure as Mr. Pickwick relieved against a background of the fighting police constables at Ipswich or the roaring mobs of Eatanswill. Of the degeneration of the Wellers, though it has been commonly assumed by critics, I am not so sure. Some of the things said in the humorous assembly round Mr. Weller's Watch are really human and laughable and altogether in the old manner. Especially, I think, the vague and awful allusiveness of old Mr. Weller when he reminds his little grandson of his delinquencies under the trope or figure of their being those of another little boy, is really in the style both of the irony and the domesticity of the poorer classes. Sam also says one or two things really worthy of himself. We feel almost as if Sam were a living man, and could not appear for an instant without being amusing.

The other elements in the make-up of *Master Humphrey's Clock* come under the same paradox which I have applied to the whole work. Though not very important in literature they are somehow quite important in criticism. They show us better than anything else the whole unconscious trend of Dickens, the stuff of which his very dreams were made. If he had made up tales to amuse himself when half-awake (as I have no doubt he did) they would be just such tales as these. They would have been ghostly legends of the nooks and holes of London, echoes of old love and laughter from the taverns or the Inns of Court. In a sense also one may say that these tales are the great might-have-beens of Dickens. They are chiefly designs which he fills up here slightly and unsatisfactorily, but which he might have filled up with his own brightest and most incredible colours. Nothing, for instance, could have been nearer to the heart of Dickens than his great Gargantuan conception of Gog and Magog telling London legends to each other all through the night. Those two giants might have stood on either side of some new great city of his invention, swarming with fanciful figures and noisy with new events. But as it is, the two giants stand alone in a wilderness, guarding either side of a gate that leads nowhere.

REPRINTED PIECES

THOSE abuses which are supposed to belong specially to religion belong to all human institutions. They are not the sins of supernaturalism, but the sins of nature. In this respect it is interesting to observe that all the evils which our Rationalist or Protestant tradition associates with the idolatrous veneration of sacred figures arises in the merely human atmosphere of literature and history. Every extravagance of hagiology can be found in hero-worship. Every folly alleged in the worship of saints can be found in the worship of poets. There are those who are honourably and intensely opposed to the atmosphere of religious symbolism or religious archæology. There are people who have a vague idea that the worship of saints is worse than the imitation of sinners. There are some, like a lady I once knew, who think that hagiology is the scientific study of hags. But these slightly prejudiced persons generally have idolatries and superstitions of their own, particularly idolatries and superstitions in connection with celebrated people. Mr. Stead preserves a pistol belonging to Oliver Cromwell in the office of the *Review of Reviews;* and I am sure he worships it in his rare moments of solitude and leisure. A man, who could not be induced to believe in God by all the arguments of all the philosophers, professed himself ready to believe if he could see it stated on a postcard in the handwriting of Mr. Gladstone. Persons not otherwise noted for their religious exercise have been known to procure and preserve portions of the hair of Paderewski. Nay, by this time blasphemy itself is a sacred tradition, and almost as much respect would be paid to the alleged relics of an atheist as to the alleged relics of a god. If any one has a fork that belonged to Voltaire, he could probably exchange it in the open market for a knife that belonged to St. Theresa.

Of all the instances of this there is none stranger than the case of Dickens. It should be pondered very carefully by those who reproach Christianity with having been easily corrupted into a system of superstitions. If ever there was a message full of what modern people call true Christianity, the direct appeal to the common heart, a faith that was simple, a hope that was infinite, and a charity that was omnivorous, if ever there came among men what they call the Christianity of Christ, it was in the message of Dickens. Christianity has been in the world nearly two thousand years, and it has not yet quite lost, its enemies being judges, its first fire and charity; but friends and enemies would agree that it was from the very first more detailed and doctrinal than the spirit of Dickens. The spirit of Dickens has been in the world about sixty years; and already it is a superstition. Already it is loaded with relics. Already it is stiff with antiquity.

Everything that can be said about the perversion of Christianity can be said about the perversion of

Dickens. It is said that Christ's words are repeated by the very High Priests and Scribes whom He meant to denounce. It is just as true that the jokes in *Pickwick* are quoted with delight by the very bigwigs of bench and bar whom Dickens wished to make absurd and impossible. It is said that texts from Scripture are constantly taken in vain by Judas and Herod, by Caiaphas and Annas. It is just as true that texts from Dickens are rapturously quoted on all our platforms by Podsnap and Honeythunder, by Pardiggle and Veneering, by Tigg when he is forming a company, or Pott when he is founding a newspaper. People joke about Bumble in defence of Bumbledom; people allude playfully to Mrs. Jellyby while agitating for Borrioboola Gha. The very things which Dickens tried to destroy are preserved as relics of him. The very houses he wished to pull down are propped up as monuments of Dickens. We wish to preserve everything of him, except his perilous public spirit.

This antiquarian attitude towards Dickens has many manifestations, some of them somewhat ridiculous. I give one startling instance out of a hundred of the irony remarked upon above. In his first important book, Dickens lashed the loathsome corruption of our oligarchical politics, their blaring servility and dirty diplomacy of bribes, under the name of an imaginary town called Eatanswill. If Eatanswill, wherever it was, had been burned to the ground by its indignant neighbours the day after the exposure, it would have been not inappropriate. If it had been entirely deserted by its inhabitants, if they had fled to hide themselves in holes and caverns, one could have understood it. If it had been struck by a thunderbolt out of heaven or outlawed by the whole human race, all that would seem quite natural. What has really happened is this: that two respectable towns in Suffolk are still disputing for the honour of having been the original Eatanswill; as if two innocent hamlets each claimed to be Gomorrah. I make no comment; the thing is beyond speech.

But this strange sentimental and relic-hunting worship of Dickens has many more innocent manifestations. One of them is that which takes advantage of the fact that Dickens happened to be a journalist by trade. It occupies itself therefore with hunting through papers and magazines for unsigned articles which may possibly be proved to be his. Only a little time ago one of these enthusiasts ran up to me, rubbing his hands, and told me that he was sure he had found two and a half short paragraphs in *All the Year Round* which were certainly written by Dickens, whom he called (I regret to say) the Master. Something of this archæological weakness must cling to all mere reprints of his minor work. He was a great novelist; but he was also, among other things, a good journalist and a good man. It is often necessary for a good journalist to write bad literature. It is sometimes the first duty of a good man to write it. Pot-boilers to my feeling are sacred things; but they may well be secret as well as sacred, like the holy pot which it is their purpose to boil. In the collection called *Reprinted Pieces* there are some, I think, which demand or deserve this apology. There are many which fall below the level of his recognised books of fragments, such as *The*

Sketches by Boz, and *The Uncommercial Traveller*.
Two or three elements in the compilation, however,
make it quite essential to any solid appreciation of the
author.

Of these the first in importance is that which comes
last in order. I mean the three remarkable pamphlets
upon the English Sunday, called *Sunday under Three
Heads*. Here, at least, we find the eternal Dickens,
though not the eternal Dickens of fiction. His other
political and sociological suggestions in this volume are
so far unimportant that they are incidental, and even
personal. Any man might have formed Dickens's
opinion about flogging for garrotters, and altered it
afterwards. Any one might have come to Dickens's
conclusion about model prisons, or to any other conclusion equally reasonable and unimportant. These
things have no colour of the great man's character.
But on the subject of the English Sunday he does stand
for his own philosophy. He stands for a particular
view, remote at present both from Liberals and Conservatives. He was, in a conscious sense, the first of
its spokesmen. He was in every sense the last.

In his appeal for the pleasures of the people, Dickens
has remained alone. The pleasures of the people have
now no defender, Radical or Tory. The Tories despise
the people. The Radicals despise the pleasures.

THE END